PAWS, PURPOSE
and **POSSIBILITIES**

To Laney ~
Gail Siwotters
6-26-22

PAWS, PURPOSE and **POSSIBILITIES**

*how therapy dogs
and faith healed
my heart*

Gail Scoates

Published by Grato Publishing Company

Paws, Purpose and Possibilities (How Therapy Dogs and Faith Healed My Heart)
Copyright © 2022 Gail Scoates
Photography by David Scoates

ISBN – Paperback 979-8-9859562-0-7
ISBN – e-book 979-8-9859562-1-4
ISBN – Hardcover 979-8-9859562-2-1

All rights reserved. No part of this publication may be reproduced, distributed, or transmitted in any form or by any means, including photocopying, recording, or other electronic or mechanical methods, without the prior written permission of the publisher, except in the case of brief quotations embodied in critical reviews and certain other noncommercial uses permitted by copyright law.

Although the author and publisher have made every effort to ensure that the information in this book was correct at press time, the author and publisher do not assume and hereby disclaim any liability to any party for any loss, damage, or disruption, caused by errors or omissions, whether such errors or omissions result from negligence, accident or any other cause. The names of a few people have been changed to protect their privacy.

All Scriptures unless otherwise indicated, are taken from the Holy Bible, New International Version®, NIV®. Copyright © 1973, 1978, 1984, 2011 by Biblica, Inc.™ Used by permission of Zondervan. All rights reserved worldwide. www.zondervan.com The "NIV" and "New International Version" are trademarks registered in the United States Patent and Trademark Office by Biblica, Inc.®

Scripture quotations marked (NLT) are taken from the Holy Bible, New Living Translation, copyright © 1996, 2004, 2007 by Tyndale House Foundation. Used by permission of Tyndale House Publishers, Inc., Carol Stream, IL 60188. All rights reserved.

I dedicate this book and my work with therapy dogs to my sister, Karen, who helped define who I am today.

I thank God every day for his ongoing work in my life.

And . . . I am grateful for therapy dogs everywhere and those who work with them.

Table of Contents

Preface	1
PART ONE Dogs and More Dogs	7
Chapter 1: The Newspaper	9
Chapter 2: Unexpected Blessings	21
Chapter 3: Karen's Journey	33
PART TWO Therapy Dogs	55
Chapter 4: Pets Are Working Saints	57
Chapter 5: PAWS Stories	69
Chapter 6: Miss Tucker	79
Chapter 7: Becoming a Therapy Dog	89
Chapter 8: Mellow Max	105
Chapter 9: Max Visits	113
Chapter 10: Getting Started	123
Chapter 11: Go-Live	133
Chapter 12: Sadie	149
PART THREE Looking Back	169
Chapter 13: Dogs Make a Difference	171
Chapter 14: Therapy Dog Evaluator	181
Chapter 15: Memorable Moments	193
Chapter 16: Always a Therapy Dog	207
Acknowledgments	223
Author Bio	227
Endnotes	229

Preface

I am writing this book for my sister, Karen. I stayed with Karen for the last four months of her life as she lived courageously with colon cancer. During those months, I saw the love of her family as we all cared for and loved her on her journey to heaven. Paramount to those who loved her were her two golden retrievers, Preston and Tanner. They joyfully stayed by her side and loved her unconditionally. They showed up at just the right time, whenever she needed them, and they knew just what to do to bring her unmistakable joy in the moment. This is about my journey with therapy dogs for over twenty years. This is my gift to Karen. I did not see then, nor many times along this long journey, how God was present and interceded at each moment. But I see it now.

At the time of Karen's diagnosis, I'd been a nurse for nearly twenty years. For many of those years, I'd worked in hospice. I'd seen lots of loss and thought I understood it. But the loss of my sister when she was forty-one years old was unimaginable. The depth of my sorrow was like being at the bottom of a deep stone quarry and wondering how I was going to get out. How does one go on with life when part of the life that defined them is no longer there?

Elizabeth Kubler-Ross, considered by some to be the guru of grief, describes the stages of grief as denial, anger, bargaining, depression and acceptance.[1] I recall thinking about her work as I was grieving and found myself experiencing what I'd taught others and what I'd seen in my hospice work. No two people experience grief in the same way. Some don't experience all the stages and others get stuck in one stage and are only able to move forward years later, maybe with counseling or medication. In her original work, Kubler-Ross suggested the last stage of healthy grieving is acceptance. This is supposedly when the person grieving accepts the reality of the loss of their loved one and is ready to move on with life. But it's a new life, a life that is forever changed.

A recent concept developed by Kubler-Ross's coauthor now suggests there is a sixth stage of grief he calls "finding meaning." This was a new concept for me. But as I began to think about and write this book, I came to realize that finding meaning in my loss was what I had been searching for all along; I knew what I was doing was to honor Karen, something positive in light of the negative I'd experienced. Those many years ago, I understood that whatever I did was never going to change the reality that Karen was gone, but I craved something to help me honor her life and move on from her death, from losing that part of me that was a Karen connection. I believe I found this meaning in my work with therapy dogs.

I knew we were doing something special with our therapy dog work. I kept notes for all my dog activities throughout my work; maybe I knew that one day I would tell someone what I did and why I did it. I have the names of most of those who participated and notes that I wrote as we did our visits. When I retired, Pam—instrumental in parts of my story—gave me a journal with a wonderful and encouraging note to look back and see the parts of my life for which I was the most grateful. I wrote notes in that journal from which many of the stories in this book are recalled.

In many ways, I've always felt a bit different from others. I've been blessed with many good and gracious things, but one of those blessings is not the stable, routine, standard family life I see in others. I understand that when I look around, I only see the outside of those lives, while I know nothing about the realities inside. But from the outside, I see myself as different. We moved away from my extended family when I was five years old. I had lived in fourteen homes by the time I got married at the age of twenty-five. My husband and I moved five times in fifteen years before we finally settled long-term in our home. I feel as though I've led a bit of a nomadic life.

Looking back, while many of the moves were good, there was always loss: loss of family, friends, jobs, stability and consistency. Other loss in my life includes a life without children, first by choice but ultimately by circumstances. Then the loss of my only sister, my father's death to suicide and my mother's sudden death at age seventy-seven. These are much less traumatic than many have experienced, but it's enough to understand what losing those you love feels like. My work in hospice on and off in my nursing career has allowed me to see how loss affects others. I work part-time in hospice today because I feel an affinity for others experiencing loss: I understand the personal and professional side of this work.

Throughout it all, I've had my faith. Stronger at times but always there. I knew long ago that I could only face my losses with faith to sustain me. As I move further into my life, I have a newfound need for a more personal relationship with the Lord. In my search for a closer walk with the Lord, I felt a nudge to share my story and my faith as a part of this journey.

As I wrote this book, I thought about my life and how it's transpired. I found my need to write this book was like having all the ingredients for a recipe but not being able to find the recipe and, therefore, no instructions on how to put it together. As I recalled each event during my writing, I smiled as well as shed tears. Tears came as I thought about and remembered my time with Karen at the end of her life. I was motivated to complete this book while Sadie, my current therapy dog, is still with me. She provides me with the love I need to work up the courage and physical as well as emotional strength to tell my story. I recalled with great joy my years with therapy dog work: starting with PAWS in 1999 to the day we moved in 2019, and my work with Karing Partners from 2010 to 2019. I am thrilled beyond the stars that Judy plans to move ahead with PAWS and Michelle has taken over Karing Partners—special ladies you will meet in my book. Because of their love for this work, these programs will continue to bring love, hope, joy, compassion, blessings and other possibilities to those they serve with this very special gift of dogs.

PART ONE

Dogs and More Dogs

The way to love anything is to realize that it might be lost.

—Gilbert K. Chesterton

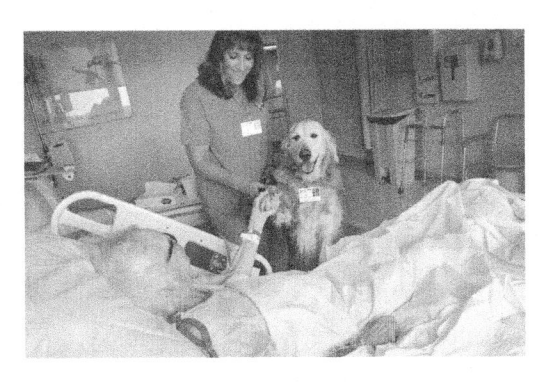

A Karing Partner visit by Michelle with Max at the hospital
(Courtesy of the *Pantagraph*)[2]

Chapter 1: The Newspaper

We're all set and waiting, waiting for *the* call. Sadie (my current therapy dog) and I are sitting on the floor with the phone nearby. We're fluffed, buffed, bathed and teeth are brushed. Our name tags and the rest of our attire are all organized, and we're waiting with bated breath.

The phone rings. It's the manager of the volunteer department, the call we've been expecting. She organized today's adventure. "It's a go!" she confirms. "Two o'clock today, we'll meet in the lobby as planned."

I get off the phone and start calling those who'll be there today. A total of four therapy dog teams, handler and dog, are in the group today. Sadie and I are one of the teams, and we are ready.

Sadie's a four-year-old golden retriever, one of the two big dogs. The other big dog team is Michelle with Max, another golden retriever who's about five years old. The small dogs are Mary with Sissy, a two-year-old Shih Tzu, and then there's Ruth with Sophie, a five-year-old Havanese. The local newspaper is sending a writer and a photographer to watch us in action today. We're excited! We put in a great deal of effort as therapy dog teams because we believe our work is important. But to think the entire hospital and local community think what we do is good work—good enough to write a story about it—that's an event to celebrate!

I make the first call to Michelle, the only one in the group working today. As soon as she answers, I tell her, "I got the call; we're all set for two o'clock today, in the lobby."

"I'll finish up here right away and get on the road," Michelle responds. "Max is ready to go. I gave him his bath last night and gave him a good talking-to about staying clean. He better not pull one of his stunts and go rolling in the dirt before we head out. I had to give him another bath before we visited last time! I have everything out and ready to go. Let's hope the traffic is good and I'm back here on time or even early, in case of any last-minute changes."

Chapter 1: The Newspaper

Michelle and I both work at the hospital. A few of the other handlers also work, but most of our therapy dog people are retired. Nice, because they're more flexible with their visits. We're all volunteers. There are other ways we could volunteer at the hospital, but we all think this is the best. Besides, we love hanging out with our dogs.

Today's my day off. On the days I volunteer with Sadie, I drive home to pick up Sadie and drive back again to the hospital. Occasionally, my husband brings Sadie to town if he has errands. Neither Michelle nor I mind the drive to pick up our dogs. It's just what we do because we love our therapy dog work!

It's time for me to call each team individually. I don't want to text or email; I want to call just in case anyone has last-minute questions. And I don't want anybody to back out.

Mary and Sissy will be there. Mary told me she can't wait to tell her story. She's been part of our group for just a short time, but her heart is truly in it! Mary was a recipient of our services while she was hospitalized and vowed if she was ever able, she wanted to participate in therapy dog work here at the hospital. She told me she talked her husband into getting her a puppy as motivation to work toward recovering.

Ruth and Sophie will also be there. They joined shortly after the start-up of the program. Ruth has a background in health education, so she's comfortable being in the hospital environment. Like all the other teams, Ruth and Sophie are special and bring their unique skills to their visits. Ruth submitted an article to a therapy dog magazine about an experience she and Sophie had, and it was published! This is a story I'm sure Ruth will tell the newspaper today.

With phone calls completed, Sadie and I start getting ready. We had spa day yesterday which included Sadie's bath, rub down and a good brushing. I brush her teeth before every visit and she *loves* that. She doesn't particularly like her bath, but she tolerates it because she knows that she's "going to work." I'm wearing my green volunteer shirt and name tag.

"C'mon, Sadie, we gotta get ready to go visit," I call to her as I get up and walk to the other room. She runs into the living room where we have all of her "work clothes."

We keep our attire in a special cabinet. She comes and sits right in front of me and waits to get prepped. I replace her regular collar with a special collar and scarf for working. Her scarf matches my shirt. The final item is her name tag. She has a regular volunteer name tag with her name and picture on it, just like mine, and people love checking it out. They've never seen a dog with an official name tag before. Sadie's

Chapter 1: The Newspaper

on her best behavior as we get ready. I truly believe she's aware of the joy she brings to everyone she visits, wherever she goes. After a quick look-over of both of us, I grab a pen to jot down notes, put hand sanitizer in my pocket, and we're off.

Driving to town, Sadie sits and gazes out the back window. She looks around at the scenery going by. It's a thirty-minute drive. Sometimes she takes a quick power nap on the way, but not today. Excitement is welling up in me like I'm going to explode, so I keep talking and talking. I tell her all that we're going to do, and, of course, I believe she knows what I'm saying. As we near our destination, she starts to get excited. She puts her nose up to the top of the window, which is her cue for me to open the window slightly so she can sniff the air. She knows we're getting close to the hospital. As we pull into the parking lot, she stands and her tail starts to wag. She knows we're here!

Before we get out of the car, I try to get organized. I usually leave my purse in the car, so I stuff it under the seat. Now, where are my keys? Okay, they go in my pocket. There's my fanny pack for those items that won't all fit in my pockets. Sadie gives me a look that says, "Are you ready yet?"

Once I get myself put together, we get out and head to the entrance. Sadie sniffs around and checks things out in the parking lot. Often, we run into folks in the parking lot who want to stop and talk and pet, but today we manage to make it in without any unexpected delays.

We enter the main entrance and walk to the volunteer sign-in office. This is where we store our personal things while we're working. After signing in, we walk to the lobby to meet our team members and the people from the newspaper. If today is like most days, we'll encounter delays from visitors and staff who want to stop and pet Sadie and talk about their dogs as we make our way to our destination. I normally love to tell my story to those who don't know about our therapy dog work. Truth be told, I also just like talking to the people I know. Everyone loves when the dogs come to visit. But today I'm in a bit of a hurry, and I start to get fidgety. I don't want to be late. We finally make it to the lobby where we meet the others.

The volunteer manager is here along with members of the hospital's marketing department. The marketing department instigated today's happenings. There was a newspaper article printed back in 2004 when Max (my first therapy dog) and I were visiting another part of the hospital. The marketing group thought an updated story with our many additional therapy dog members and updated stories was warranted. Paul is here again from the newspaper. He wrote the prior story, and he's going

Chapter 1: The Newspaper

to interview us today. A photographer is also here.

As we arrive, the other therapy dog teams are getting settled and ready for the afternoon. They huddle and talk with the photographer while Sadie and I say our hellos to Paul. Paul remembers me from years ago when he did the article about me and Max. It's good to see him again. And he's pleased to meet Sadie today.

Paul begins, "I'm looking forward to this afternoon and hanging out with you and the dogs. I want to talk with you separately from the others before we get started so I understand better what you're doing and why you're doing this."

Paul and Sadie and I settle in a corner of the lobby where we can talk somewhat unobstructed. Sadie's a bit perplexed at not being able to hang with her doggie friends, but she settles nicely as Paul and I talk.

He begins the conversation. "I recall coming to take pictures, and we did an interview several years ago. But if I remember right, it was only you and one other dog. Today there's a larger group of people and dogs. I'm interested in knowing what's happened in the past few years and what makes the doggie program different from what it was years ago."

So I tell him my story. I remind him I've been doing therapy dog work for many years here at the hospital, and even years before I met Paul for our first interview.

I tell him, "You met Max a few years ago when he was about ten years old. He was a certified therapy dog, but we did not have an official program back then. It was just me and Max coming to visit. Sadly, he's no longer with us. Today I'm here with Sadie. She's my third therapy dog. Sadie, as well as all the dogs working today, is a certified therapy dog. We're all certified through one of the national therapy dog associations. We go through lots of training and testing to make sure they behave as well as they're behaving today. Do you notice how well the dogs get along with the other dogs? One of the important traits of a therapy dog is that they're pretty mellow, they listen to their 'person' and they like people. Many therapy dogs even prefer people over dogs. They're trained to just hang out and not play with the other dogs while they're working."

I remind him of the work I did with Max on the transitional care unit years ago. I explain, "Max and I were invited to come and visit that unit as part of their activity program. Once we received the okay to visit, Max and I visited once or twice a month. That's when you met us years ago.

"Then one day when I was working, one of the nurses stopped to ask me about what Max and I were doing. So I told her and she said, 'When are you going to start doing visits in the rest of the hospital?'" I went on to tell

Chapter 1: The Newspaper

Paul what we did to start the program and how we got to where we are today.

"Where did you come up with the name Karing Partners?" he inquires. He points out I have the word spelled differently, *caring* starting with a K instead of a C, and he tells me it intrigues him.

"When I met you and Max years ago," he notes, "and I wrote a similar article, it was just you and Max making visits. I don't recall a name for the work you were doing at the time."

I should have known he was going to ask me this. Why was I not more prepared? As I talk, the tears start. How can the tears still come after so many years? The calendar says it was a long time ago. But my heart says it was yesterday. How can the hurt still be there after so long?

"Why did I do this? I did this for a purpose," I tell him. "You see, my sister's name is Karen. She's in heaven now. I lived with her for the last four months of her life, and I cared for her. I watched as her two golden retrievers provided loving 'therapy' to her throughout that time. It seemed as if they knew she was getting sicker. Their behavior changed as her needs changed. It seemed that they were able to be whatever it was she needed at the moment.

"It took me many years to grieve and be involved in therapy dog work in other settings before I was able to

17

do this full-scale work at the hospital. But when the opportunity presented itself to start a program here, I said yes. But it had to be named Karing Partners, named after Karen."

I tell him how my love of dogs started in childhood, and how my nursing career instilled in me a love for people and a desire to work with people. After Karen died, I wanted to do something positive, something loving in her memory. Like so many others, I wanted to find meaning in her suffering and my grief, to find a time and place where I could again experience acceptance and hope. When circumstances fell into place to bring these life events together, I found myself on a journey I never could have imagined.

So I told him my story. And now I'll tell you.

Paws for Reflection

God can take times of grief and heartbreak and turn them around. Dare I say turn them into joy? In the moment, this would never seem possible. But given time and God's goodness, he can turn our grief around. Numerous examples in the Bible reveal how God took sad or bad situations and turned them into something good. Consider the story of Joseph and his eleven brothers. Joseph's brothers attempted to kill him by tossing him into a well, and then later sold him into slavery. Yet many years later, not only did Joseph survive but God turned his situation around, and Joseph saved his brothers and their families from the famine in Egypt.

I believe God did this for me. After Karen died, he took my broken heart and turned it into a joy-filled journey of work with therapy dogs. "For his anger lasts only a moment, but his favor lasts a lifetime; weeping may last through the night, but rejoicing comes with the morning" (Psalm 30:5).

And God knows us; he knows the gifts and talents he has given us. If we are open, he will place us on a pathway to use those gifts and talents to serve people and find the joy we seek. He took my background in nursing, my love of people and my love of dogs and put them together for the best possible outcome. I believe he gives us choices and allows us to choose what path to take. "You should do as I have done for you" (John 13:15). As we serve others, it not only blesses them but also brings tremendous joy to our lives.

Have you experienced loss or grief? Are you ready to embark on a journey from this place to find meaning and hope? Have you looked into opportunities in which to engage where you might find meaning? Have you pursued a place to dwell where others might understand your grief? It is possible for God to place on your heart the potential to find joy despite your grief. With faith, it is possible to find meaning in your grief, to ease the pain of your loss and serve others.

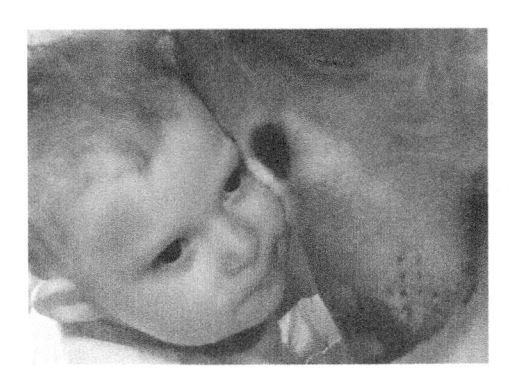

Eva, Karen's granddaughter, with Max

Chapter 2: Unexpected Blessings

Most of us recall our first encounter with a dog. It may have been the family dog, the dog that belonged to Cousin Joe, or the one that lived with the kids down the block. Hopefully, most are good memories. I suspect some, though, have memories that aren't so good. Like my cousin, who was bit by a dog when she was young, and from then on would have nothing to do with dogs. That is, until one of her kids grew up, got a dog, and she proceeded to fall in love with it.

My dad's parents had lots of dogs. I enjoyed hearing the stories about dogs and their antics of when my dad was a kid. I still have a picture of my dad as a young man with a rifle and his hunting dog, a Spaniel named

Jack. Dad would tell all sorts of stories about his dogs, especially Jack. That's when I knew I wanted a dog.

I was the big sister, and Karen was three years younger. We moved often as kids and were always the new kids on the block. When I was seven, we moved to Ohio, many miles away from our family in Wisconsin. I felt different from the other kids. We had no cousins or grandparents nearby like the other families in our new neighborhood. It was just the four of us: me and Karen, my mom and dad.

But it all changed when I was in the fifth grade. It happened one day when Karen and I got home after school. We noticed it was quieter than usual. Mom was working the afternoon shift, her usual shift as a nurse at the factory. Dad usually got home shortly after we arrived. It was an eerie silence, one that did not feel comfortable. Suddenly, we heard a noise.

"What was that?" Karen asked apprehensively.

"I don't know," I replied. I didn't know what the noise was, and I was a bit nervous too, but no way was I going to admit that. I was, after all, the big sister. But what was that strange noise? What awful thing could be lurking around the corner of the room?

We heard the noise again and both jumped. This time as we listened, we heard taps on the floor and other strange sounds. Was that whimpering? It sounded like little cries.

Then out of the back room came a little black puppy! We watched as it sniffed and meandered, unaware of its surroundings. Then the puppy saw us and came running toward us. And out from the back room came Mom and Dad.

"What do you think?" Mom asked excitedly. "She's our new little puppy."

"What!" Karen squealed. "A dog? We finally have a dog! What's her name?"

Mom said we could name her. "The people who have her parents called her Suzy. But we can call her anything you want. We can come up with a new name."

We couldn't contain our excitement. Picking up the puppy, Karen snuggled and kissed the puppy as the puppy wiggled in her arms.

"We have a dog!" Karen exclaimed. "I like Suzy. Let's just call her Suzy."

So Suzy came into our life. The first of many dogs to live with us. Suzy was a medium-sized black poodle who thought she was a princess. As our first dog, and being ever so cute, we spoiled her terribly.

But I do remember the time when she was not a princess. I'm sure she didn't feel like a princess and certainly didn't look like one. I suspect Mom and Dad, ever so aware of their budget since my dad was going to school, thought they'd save money on grooming by having one of Dad's buddies trim Suzy. What a terrible mistake. Her haircut was awful! Even Suzy knew she looked terrible. For the next few weeks, we couldn't find Suzy. Most of the time she hid under the bed. I still recall hand feeding her under the bed as she simply would not come out. I remember wondering back then, *Do dogs think?* From that time on, I was convinced dogs do have significant perception and awareness of their surroundings, especially when relating to their "pack." They pick up on our emotions and can exhibit joy and sorrow. That episode made an impact on my heart.

When Suzy was about two years old, Mom and Dad decided Suzy was lonely. Most days we were all gone at school and work, leaving Suzy alone. One day Mom asked me and Karen, "What do you think about getting another dog? The lady where we got Suzy called and said there will be some more puppies coming soon. Would you like another puppy?"

What a silly question. Of course, we'd like another puppy! We planned a family outing to see the puppies a few weeks later to pick out the puppy we wanted. Since Karen was the youngest, we decided to let her pick out our dog. We'd already decided we wanted a little male puppy. So on this particular day, we went to select which male puppy we wanted to bring home.

"How am I going to pick out our dog?" Karen asked quizzically.

"Just go in and sit down by the puppies. Let's see which doggie comes to you," my mom instructed.

We arrived at the farm where the dogs lived. The lady met us at the door and took us to the puppy enclosure. Karen crawled into the melee of puppies that were eagerly jumping all about. As we watched, a little male puppy came over to Karen and climbed right into her lap. "I think we should take this one." She smiled and looked up at us. We all agreed this was our puppy. From that point forward, my parents never had less than two dogs.

We took the puppy home and named him Andy. We were excited about the new addition to our family; however, Suzy definitely did not share our excitement. As we introduced them, it was clear that Suzy was not too keen on the idea of a puppy in her kingdom. After all, she was the princess. Apparently, a princess should not have to put up with all this puppy activity.

But as with many things in life, good things come to those who wait. So it was with Andy and Suzy. Andy settled down and Suzy made sure he was aware of her standing as top dog. Andy was absolutely in love with Suzy and so his standing as second-in-command worked just fine with him. Andy was one of those dogs that was a pleasure to be around. Suzy and Andy. They were always together. Andy, always the gentleman, let Suzy take the lead in anything she wanted. Who says dogs don't think!

We loved our dogs so much we reckoned everyone needed a dog! Let me be precise, *my mother* thought everyone needed a dog. She decided her brother and his family ought to have a dog. So since Andy was young and not yet neutered, we had Andy mated with a small black poodle. We got the pick of the litter. For Christmas that year, we drove Andy's puppy nearly five hundred miles to my aunt and uncle in Oshkosh, Wisconsin. Karen and I and the puppy slept most of the way in the back seat. It was our job to keep him quiet and entertained. We gave Fritzie, named after my dad, to my uncle for Christmas that year. Fritzie was a bit of a wild man, and one of his greatest joys in life was to run, especially run away to my grandparents' house, where he was immediately reprimanded and brought back home. Like Suzy and Andy, Fritzie became another loved and spoiled dog.

When I turned twelve, we moved to a house where my bedroom was downstairs while Karen and my mom and dad had bedrooms upstairs. Since the dogs both slept with Mom and Dad, I was alone on the first floor. My parents were a bit worried about me being scared or lonely and they asked me if I was nervous about being alone downstairs.

"I'm just fine," I lied. While I hadn't given much thought to this idea, I started to remember nights I was sort of scared and lonely being the only one downstairs after everyone else went to bed.

But something was about to change. It was Christmas morning. I was lying in bed thinking about the day before and the gifts we'd opened on Christmas Eve. I was suddenly jarred to attention by the rapid puttering of footsteps in the hallway. They stopped right outside my bedroom door. Then hammering on the door, a million tap tap taps all at once, it was like a jackhammer pounding into the ground.

"You have to get up right now and come out here," Karen shouted as she knocked. "You just gotta see this." She was talking as fast as she'd been tapping on my bedroom door.

I got up and ran with her into the living room. *What's the big deal?* We'd opened our gifts last night. That was our family tradition, open gifts after church on Christmas Eve. I couldn't imagine what this was about.

Sitting next to the Christmas tree was a big box with a huge red ribbon. As we peered over the top, we could see there were holes in the top of the box. As we inched ever so close, we heard whimpering sounds. *Could it be? Is it possible?*

Karen opened the box with great enthusiasm. "I think it's a puppy!" she said excitedly. "There's a puppy in the box! And look, here's your name!" As I opened the box, out popped an energetic little black puppy.

Just then, Mom and Dad showed up with Suzy and Andy. "What's this noise all about?" my dad said gruffly. As if he didn't know! By that time, the puppy was running around and making all sorts of happy puppy sounds and jumping all over the place. Karen and I joined the puppy dance. I looked at Suzy and Andy, who were staring tentatively at this strange creature making all sorts of noises. They were clearly not excited and looked at us as if to say, "Are you kidding me?"

How my parents managed to keep this puppy a secret from me and Karen, I'll never know! Since he was my dog, I got to name him. It was easy. I'd had many stuffed dogs over the years, and they were all named Tige. Not too original, I guess. But truth be told, even at the old age of twelve, I was still sleeping with my most recent Tige. For some reason, I'd fallen in love with the name after seeing an old Buster Brown ad. Buster Brown was a child character in shoe sales ads in the early 1900s. His best buddy was his dog named Tige. Somehow, as a young child, I'd latched onto one of those pictures and connected with the dog and his name. So when I saw my very own real dog, I just knew his name was Tige.

Tige became my best friend. I told him all my secrets; I told him everything and knew he'd never rat on me. Tige slept with me every night. Tige took his job quite seriously as my keeper. He did not like when I had friends over because they distracted me from him; I think he was jealous! As I got older and boyfriends would visit, Tige took it upon himself to chaperone us. Mom and Dad loved that he'd hang out with us and sit on my lap and want attention the entire time the boys were there. I still recall being totally dismayed when Tige brought out one of my bras when my date was there. Oh, utter dismay! How embarrassing for a sixteen-year-old girl! But Mom and Dad loved it and never let me forget that story.

After Suzy and Andy and Tige came Jackie. Jackie was a brown poodle but a bit bigger than the other dogs. He made it clear he was the alpha dog. But he was also Karen's dog. He was her best friend and constant companion. Karen later told me stories similar to mine about how Jackie was always right there, especially when boyfriends were around. Like he was spying on her and her friends. We both agreed: our parents used those dogs as watchdogs to chaperone us.

When I went to college, Suzy was gone, but Andy, Tige and Jackie were still at home. But it was never the same again. Tige became best friends with my dad. And eventually Jackie became my dad's best friend too, after Karen moved away. Mom and Dad continued to have two or three dogs at a time for the remainder of their lives. Mom's last dog, another Andy, lived until just a year before she passed away. Yes, dogs were a big part of our life growing up.

In honor of National Kids Day, The Drake Center for Veterinary Care looked at kids: those who lived with dogs and those who lived without dogs. They wanted to know if there were advantages for kids who grow up with dogs. The results showed it was good for kids to have a dog. They found kids with dogs are more responsible, have a healthy immune system, show emotional intelligence and compassion, have more self-esteem, are more active and secure, are better able to cope with isolation and depression, show reduced anxiety, and more.[3]

Paws for Reflection

God gives good gifts to his children. One of the greatest gifts he gives is his love for us. "Every good and perfect gift is from above, coming down from the Father of the heavenly lights, who does not change like shifting shadows" (James 1:17). Writers of the Bible want us to know that every good thing in our life is a gift from God. This verse from James also reminds us that God is always present as the light in our life.

I believe one of the good gifts God gives us is our dogs. Dogs do wonderful things for the soul. They love us. They forgive us even when we may mistreat them or not love them back the way they love us. They are our constant companions. For many dogs, their main purpose in life is to love us and make us happy. What a good deal we got when God placed dogs in our lives to show us how to truly love his creatures. I think our dogs reflect what the Bible says in 1 John 4:7–8: "Dear friends, let us love one another, for love comes from God. Everyone who loves has been born of God and knows God. Who does not love does not know God, because God is love."

What unexpected blessings, what good gifts has God given you? Think about what you have to be grateful for today. If you have never done so, make a list of the good things in your life. Review that list and think about how God is good and has blessed you. Can you give him thanks today?

Gail (left) and Karen at Christmas the year we got our golden retriever puppies

Chapter 3: Karen's Journey

Roger Caras, a wildlife photographer and television personality, once said, "If you don't own a dog, at least one, there is not necessarily anything wrong with you, but there may be something wrong with your life."[4] Our family took to heart Roger's proclamation! It's no coincidence, therefore, to learn that Karen and I went on to have dogs in our adult lives. And just as when we were children, the dogs in our adult lives continued to provide us with love and companionship.

Karen got a dog shortly after she was married. Truth be told, Mom and Dad gave Karen and her new husband a puppy. You notice a trend, right? My mother gave lots of people lots of dogs. Like all our other dogs as kids, Tobias Jacque was a small brown toy poodle. TJ for short.

A few years went by and Karen called me. "We're moving to a place where TJ can run outside and I don't have to take him out all the time. We're looking for a small house with a fenced-in yard so Shannon and TJ can play safely in the backyard. Now that Shannon's two years old, I want her and TJ to be in a safe place when they're outside."

Shortly after the call, they moved into a little two-bedroom house in the suburbs with a fenced-in backyard. It was just what they were looking for. They settled into the neighborhood. One thing the neighbors soon learned about Karen was her love for animals.

Karen became known as the Animal Lady. On numerous occasions, she'd call me and tell me she'd taken in yet another critter after a call where she learned about an animal needing a home. Or she'd wake up in the morning to find one left on the front porch. She found homes for most of them, but a few she kept.

"We got another doggie today. I think she's an older puppy, about a year or two years old. A black and white mix of some kind, maybe a cross with a poodle," Karen said in a spirited tone on the phone.

"What are you going to do with this one?" I asked, somewhat dubiously. She already had TJ and two cats and, of course, she was busy with Shannon, almost four years old.

"You already have Casey and Pearl and you still have TJ. What are the neighbors going to think?"

"I really don't care what they think," she said determinedly. "Anyway, they already know how I love my animals. We have a fenced-in yard, so none of them run. I'm actually thinking about keeping this one. TJ needs a friend. Anyway, I've already named her Melissa." The decision had been made.

So Melissa became part of the family. Melissa was a lovely dog and very gentle. She got along well with TJ, Casey and Pearl. All was well. For the moment.

Soon, along came Charlie. He came into their lives when Shannon was five years old. Shannon was playing outside. She crossed the street and was hit by a car. Thankfully, her injuries were not life-threatening but enough to send the family into a jitter. So what does an animal-loving family do to console their daughter? Get her a puppy, of course!

Charlie was a black and white mix that Shannon's dad found on the street. He decided this puppy was good medicine for Shannon's recovery. Charlie was a lover, but Charlie was a hoodlum! He loved it when everyone was home and assigned himself to be Shannon's best friend. He got used to having people home as Shannon recovered but didn't like it when everyone went back to work and school. Charlie decided he didn't like being left alone, so one day when everyone was gone, Charlie chewed up the couch and a few other things. After that, Charlie was kenneled when everyone was gone. Charlie eventually settled down to be a loving, affectionate dog and no longer got in trouble.

While Karen was busy living her life with her two-legged and four-legged family, I was many states away. David and I got our first dog, Jasper, when we transferred to Chicago. Jasper was a black lab mix who kept me company while David's work often took him away from home. Jasper was a self-appointed security guard when my husband was out of town. I would leave the front curtains open just enough to let Jasper stand tall and look out the window when we were alone. Never do I recall having to ward off a salesperson because when they saw Jasper, they simply walked on by.

While we were living in Chicago, Karen and Shannon and their menagerie, along with my mom and dad, moved to Wisconsin. I was happy because we saw more of them all since they were now a bit closer. In the fall of 1993, Karen called to tell me she was struggling with the decision to put TJ down. He was nearly fifteen years old, could not see or hear and could hardly walk. "I know what I need to do, but I just can't do it," she said dismally. With support and encouragement, she finally made the difficult decision.

I called her a week later and told her my sad news. Our Jasper, only eleven years old, had suddenly become sick over the weekend, and we had no choice but to put him down immediately. We cried and shared our losses. We'd both been talking to our parents about what we were going through. As usual, Mom had the answer. My parents offered to get each of us a puppy for Christmas that year.

"What do you think we should get?" Karen asked excitedly. We were living about two hundred miles apart, so all our conversations were by phone. Were we going to get the same breed, were we going to get different-sized dogs, or what? Karen was open to either a small or large dog, but I was leaning toward another big dog.

"I loved having a big dog," I said. "I know you and I had small dogs when we were kids, but I want another big dog. And we both have large fenced-in yards, so we can handle big dogs."

We did our homework. I was the first to make a decision. David and I agreed we wanted a golden retriever. We'd done some checking around. Golden retrievers were the size we were looking for and were known to be good with children and other dogs. I talked to Karen about what we'd decided and why. She thought about this long and hard because Shannon was still at home, as well as the two cats and Charlie. In the end, she decided she would also get a golden retriever.

Mom started checking around for golden retriever puppies that would be ready for a home in the late fall. Mom and Karen found a breeder about twenty miles from where they lived and decided that was where we were going to get our Christmas dogs.

I drove up to Wisconsin a few weeks later. Mom, Karen, Shannon and I went to visit the breeder to see the four-week-old puppies. The puppies were in a special area of the basement the family had designed to house and keep the puppies. We also met the dog's mom and dad. They were lovely, mild-mannered and medium gold in color. Mom, Karen and Shannon had been there a few days earlier, and they'd picked out a little male for Karen and a female for me. So we stepped into the handmade wooden pen to play with "our" puppies.

As Karen got in the pen, her puppy came bounding up to play with her. The pup they'd selected for me was a bit shy and sat in the back. But another little female came running up to me as if to say, "I am the one for you!" So because this puppy picked me, I decided she was meant for us. We put little ribbons on our puppies so when mom and Karen went back to pick them up a few weeks later, they were able to spot our puppies.

After eleven years, we'd both forgotten how full of energy young puppies could be. Karen's Preston and my Tucker were a bit more than we were prepared for. We looked back and found the small print we'd missed earlier in our preparation: it said, "Golden retriever puppies have exceedingly high levels of energy. They must be watched and interacted with at all times. If not, they will get into a heap of trouble." We compared notes and kept each other in stitches sharing stories of their antics. One of my favorites is a picture she had of her puppy asleep in his food bowl.

On a rare occasion, Karen and I would bring Preston and Tucker to my parents' house to let them play together. Mom and Dad had a huge fenced-in backyard for the dogs. My parents' dogs, however, were a bit overwhelmed with these active and ever-growing golden retrievers and stayed as far away as they could while we were there. Karen and I loved taking our dogs and watching them run with such abandonment. They'd run at top speed, tails and snouts up, sniffing, looking and chasing something real or imagined. Their unsurpassed glee also resulted in ruts in the yard, flowerbeds ravaged, rocks displaced and other such devastation. After a few of these wonderfully wild outings, Mom and Dad decided they didn't like the clean-up that eventually was needed, and we were not encouraged to bring them over as the dogs got older.

Karen called regularly to check on Tucker.

"How is Tucker doing? Oh, excuse me, *Miss* Tucker. How is Miss Tucker?" Karen teased me.

"Calling her Miss Tucker is working better than just Tucker," I said matter-of-factly. "I'm so tired of everyone asking if she's a boy or a girl. You'd think her pink collar and small stature would give her away, but no, everybody asks."

I'd been a visiting nurse years before. One of my favorite home-care patients talked at great length about her grand-dog Tucker. I was so familiar with her Tucker, also a golden retriever, I hadn't been able to name my Tucker anything else.

I asked in return, "How's Preston doing?"

"He's coming along pretty well. He's certainly the smartest dog I've ever had. He listens so well, which I'm happy about since he is such a big boy," she remarked.

"Well, are you going to take him to school like I told you?" I had a thing about doggie obedience. I felt it was a necessity; having well-behaved dogs is like having well-behaved kids. We debated the pros and cons of taking them to doggie school. David and I had taken our first dog, Jasper, to school several times, where we learned a lot about working with big dogs. We were committed to taking Tucker to doggie school. Karen and I went back and forth and continued to be at the opposite ends of this debate. She was not interested because she felt taking Preston to obedience classes would change his personality. I argued the opposite, as I felt the classes would bring out the best in them. With well-behaved dogs, we could take them places and they'd be better behaved around others. We never did come to a consensus on this topic. Tucker went to school and Preston did not. But he was a good boy. Goldie's are known for their loving and gentle personalities and Preston came through on those traits with flying colors.

We talked at least every week and sometimes more often. I'd see her whenever I visited my mom and dad, and she and Shannon would come over to visit. Top topics of conversation were the crazy things our dogs were up to and life in general. We'd talk and laugh about living together as widowed old ladies when we were in our eighties and how we'd still chatter about our dogs.

But one day in 1994, I got a different kind of call. "I want to know what you think. I haven't talked to Mom and Dad about this; I don't want them to worry. But I've noticed some blood on my toilet tissue and I'm constipated. Do you think I should be worried about this?" I asked the routine health care questions: When did you start to notice this? Are you having any cramping or other abdominal problems? Are you having diarrhea? We both agreed an appointment with her doctor was in order. I really wasn't worried. Goodness gracious, Karen was only thirty-eight years old! We didn't have any colon problems in our family, and we convinced each other this was likely hemorrhoids and nothing to worry about. We decided to keep in close touch. But we agreed it was best not to tell our parents for now.

A few days later she called to tell me her doctor had scheduled a colonoscopy. *Really,* I thought. She's healthy as an ox. She doesn't smoke, doesn't drink and eats pretty darned well. Dear God, her daughter is only seventeen years old. And Karen had just remarried! Seemed overkill to me, but better to be safe than sorry.

A short week later, I got the call that would change my life. It had already changed hers. She was diagnosed with Stage IV colon cancer. My heart crashed. I couldn't talk. I had to get off the phone so I could break down and tell my husband the devastating news. *How could this be happening to Karen? How could this be happing to our family?*

I don't recall many details of the following months as things happened so fast. More tests, decisions to make, so much heartache to process. Surgery was scheduled to remove the mass. Her husband had just been offered a job out of town. Now what would they do?

Surgery and tests revealed they could not remove the entire mass. They also found numerous metastases. She started on chemo. The only, only, only good thing that happened at this time, at least for me, was she and her husband relocated to a suburb near Chicago. I would be able to see her more often, and hopefully she'd find good health care being near Chicago. But she was moving away from our parents, who she was very close to, and she was moving away from Shannon, who had just started college.

I visited often after they moved. Karen was so strong. She tried every drug and chemo treatment they offered to her. Whenever Karen was home, there was Preston, always by her side. If she was on the couch, he was on the couch. If she was in bed, he was in bed with her. He was such a good boy, right there wherever she was. When I would visit and she was up to it, we'd go for a short walk with Preston. Other times we simply sat and talked. If she was feeling good, we'd occasionally go out for lunch.

About a year into this, her husband decided he wanted to give her a special gift. But what do you give someone who is going through all of this? She decided she wanted a puppy, another golden retriever. That's how Tanner came to live with Karen. He brought much-needed energy and life and love into the house.

Preston and Tanner got along well, and Preston was good with the new little puppy. They played and ran all around the house. This new level of activity was a wonderful change of pace and gave Karen something other than her illness to think about. It was good for her to have so much love around her. She experienced much joy watching her dogs play and simply exude life! They were her therapy dogs at a time when she truly needed them.

In May 1997, I took a leave of absence from my job and stayed with Karen five days a week. That way I could spend time with Karen while her husband went to work, making sure they had the finances to cover all the medical expenses. It was a special time for Karen and me. As the big sister, I'd always taken care of Karen. I'd also worked as a hospice nurse for several years. So I had the skill, I had the love, but did I have the physical and emotional strength it was going to take to get through these next few months? The one thing I knew for sure is the presence of her dogs was especially important for both of us. They not only provided entertainment and lots of love, but they provided an important element of distraction and connection that we both needed.

Karen had been in the hospital because of intractable pain for a week prior to her coming home with hospice. She'd used up all her options for research and experimental medications. The doctors offered surgery, but it would only be for pain control and not for cure. She chose not to have surgery but to go home and be in her home with her family and dogs.

At first, the dogs were hesitant. We know that dogs can sense the smell and odor of cancer, a chemical change that occurs as the body acts to fight the cancer cells. Karen was not able to eat much, so the dogs were likely aware of a smell of altered body metabolism with changes in her body chemistry. She was on high doses of morphine and other medications to control her pain, and I often wondered if there was a smell the dogs were aware of from that too. She was no longer the mom they knew before she went into the hospital. But they soon got over it and returned to their silly doggie antics.

By now Tanner was full-sized. He and Preston played and played together. It was quite a site to see two large males play so well together. Never once did I see a fight between them. Preston was in charge and Tanner simply respected that. It was nice weather in June and July, so Karen and I would sit outside with the dogs in the backyard and watch them play. They'd periodically come over to check on their mom. When she was ready to go in, they went in too. Wherever Karen was, they were right there. It was quite a sight to see the three of them: Karen, Preston and Tanner all try to fit on the couch. Karen always sat on the couch so her doggies could share the space with her. As I think back, every single time I looked at Karen, she was touching one or both of her dogs, her angel dogs.

I went to Karen's every week on Sunday night and stayed until Friday. My mom wanted to be part of Karen's care, so she came up on Friday for the night. Karen's husband was her caregiver until I returned on Sunday. But the constant in Karen's life was Preston and Tanner.

August 11, 1997, arrived just like any other day. The sun was shining; it was a warm day. By now, Karen's morphine dose was incredibly high—well over 1,000 milligrams daily to control her pain. It was being administered by an epidural line in her back with a continuous portable medication pump. Despite all that medication, just two weeks before, we'd walked through Target as she had wanted to go shopping.

Shannon was coming to spend the day that day. I made breakfast and snacks for Shannon and me. Karen wasn't eating anymore, just taking sips of water. When Shannon arrived, Preston and Tanner met her at the door with tails wagging and lots of doggie smiles and whimpers to welcome her. It brought a smile to Karen's face as she watched the joy and love shared between her most precious beings, her daughter and her dogs.

We were planning a marathon movie day. I cannot recall the first movie but the second was Shannon and Karen's favorite movie, *Pretty Woman*, starring Julia Roberts and Richard Gere. I loved the movie too but obviously not like the two of them! They sat snuggled together on Karen's big recliner chair. There was plenty of room for the two of them since Karen no longer filled the chair.

As they watched the movie together, I observed them as they looked back and forth at each other, knowing the next scene and reciting almost every word of the dialogue. They'd laugh whenever they messed up the script. I watched them more than I watched the movie that day. Shannon stayed for a bit after the movie, but by then, Karen was tired and Shannon had a two-hour drive home. That evening, Karen and I giggled as we talked about how the two of them knew so much of the dialogue for that movie.

Everything changed eight hours later. I was sleeping on the couch to be near Karen and help her if needed. That night she was in pain. I increased the dose of her morphine and gave her other medications as the hospice nurses had instructed us. But the pain continued. By now her husband was up, and we were both attending to Karen's needs. But the pain continued. I suddenly realized that Karen was not going to survive this episode of pain. My heart stopped. I was on autopilot; I did what I did because of my background and because of what the hospice team had told us. Nevertheless, I was raw, like an open wound being scraped to the core. But I needed to be strong for Karen and her husband.

We continued giving medication, holding her, and being with her. I recited the Lord's Prayer, the twenty-third Psalm, and in her calmer moments, I read from the Bible. This went on for hours. We called the hospice nurse, but by the time she arrived, Karen was gone. I recall at that moment, my world stopped.

My call to Shannon to tell her that her mother was gone, after the loving day they'd just had the day before, was excruciating. How do you tell your only niece that her mom was now in heaven? I do not recall the words I used, but I still recall Shannon's screaming cries at the other end of the phone. I remember the nurses and funeral home arriving, but I do not remember more. I'd known this moment was coming, but I was unprepared for the total physical and emotional pain I'd experience.

As I look back on this time with Karen, I'm grateful beyond words that I was able to be with her. I was blessed to stay with Karen, to watch, love and care for her. We had time to talk about many things. We prayed together when the hospice chaplain visited and we took communion. The dogs were present during every event. They loved when people came to visit but especially when family came. Most importantly, Preston and Tanner were there when Karen needed them. In her final days, it was as though Preston and Tanner knew what was happening and started to grieve. I watched as they lost interest in playtime and food, and they seemed to sleep more often. They lost interest in any of the rest of us and only wanted to be right at Karen's side. It was such a gift for me to spend this time with Karen in her final months, and I was blessed to be an observer of this special love between Karen and her dogs.

Paws for Reflection: Karen's Journey

Just as joy, happiness and blessings are a part of life, so are suffering, sadness and afflictions of many kinds. How do we reconcile this? How is it possible that a good God allows sad things, bad things, to happen? Rabbi Harold Kushner asked the same when he wrote *Why Do Bad Things Happen to Good People?* following the diagnosis of his three-year-old son with progeria, a genetic disease that causes rapid aging and early death. It was many years after Karen's death when I read his book and finally found a way to understand tragedy, sadness and suffering in a different way. Those many years later, I was finally able to accept Karen's death and channel my time and emotions in a way that helped in my grief journey.

I have no magic words to say to others. Reconciling a loss such as this is a journey we must embark on for ourselves. God understands mourning. Psalm 34:18 says, "The Lord is close to the brokenhearted and saves those who are crushed in spirit." God promises, that for those who believe in him, there will be no more mourning when we get to heaven. It says in Revelation 21:4, "He will wipe every tear from their eyes. There will be no more death or mourning or crying or pain, for the old order of things has passed away."

Everyone experiences loss and grief, but it comes to us in different ways. Loss is usually thought of as the death of a loved one, but it can also be the death of a dream, an idea, or a way of life. Grief is how we respond to our loss; and it takes time to heal. The apostles Paul and Timothy wrote in 2 Corinthians 1:3–4, "Praise be to the God and Father of our Lord Jesus Christ, the Father of compassion and the God of all comfort, who comforts us in all our troubles, so that we can comfort those in any trouble with the comfort we ourselves receive from God." God comforts us in our darkest times so that we have strength to comfort and serve others during their difficult times. But we must go on. We can feed our grief, which impairs our ability to move on, or we can accept it as part of our life journey. We can even choose to express it in gratitude of the life of our lost loved one. We can choose hope in spite of our grief.

Have you experienced loss or unspeakable grief? How did you deal with it? Find trusted friends and brothers and sisters in Christ to help you in your loss. Find people close to you who can help you walk with God on your grief journey.

Miss Tucker as a puppy

Max visits with PAWS

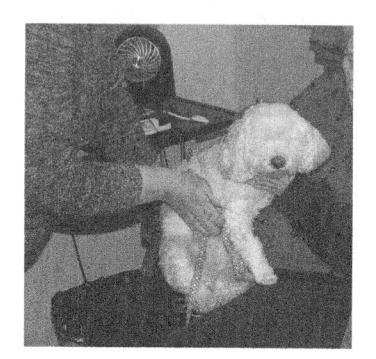

Connie with Zoey visit at the nursing home

Judy's dogs Zeta and Zeni

PAWS dogs visit at the assisted living center

Sally visits with Oreo and Bailey at the nursing home

PART TWO

Therapy Dogs

There are far, far better things ahead than any we leave behind.

—*C.S. Lewis*

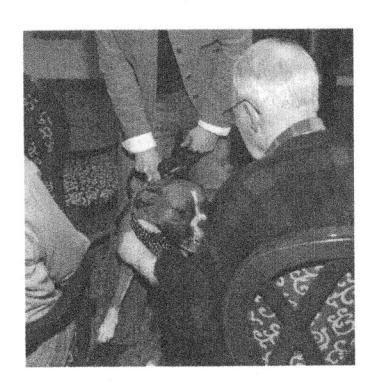

A visit with the PAWS dogs

Chapter 4: Pets Are Working Saints

I didn't know it at the time, but my faith and desire to see something good come from losing Karen would take me somewhere unexpected—on a journey of possibilities I never could have imagined—but one that over the years has come together in an amazing way and has fit so many elements of my personality and my passions in life.

Pets Are Working Saints (PAWS) is an acronym for a faith-based therapy dog program. The pastor at Wesley Church, along with one of the members with dog training experience, decided this was a good ministry for the church. They asked me to participate. But I was still a bit raw from Karen's passing. So I opted to wait awhile, till I was ready.

But it started me thinking. Therapy dog work in 1998 was in its infancy. I loved watching Animal Planet on television, so I focused on what was happening in the new and exciting therapy dog world. The more I watched, the more I knew this was something I wanted to do. I could not name the reason why, but I was enthralled. Was this something I could do? It felt like a good fit. As a nurse and dog lover, it just felt right. And I'd been there—up close and personal—watching what Preston and Tanner had done for Karen in her final days. I felt like I knew what therapy dogs could do. But still, I was not quite ready.

Tucker was almost three years old when Karen passed away. It took about two years of healing before I was ready to think about the PAWS ministry at church. Finally, after much deliberation, I decided that I would do this work, and I'd do it in memory of Karen.

I called and asked to speak with the pastor. "Hi, Pastor Hayes. This is Gail. You know the PAWS program you and Gretchen are working on? Well, I'm finally ready to get started. I think and I hope my heart has healed enough to let me give back."

"I'm happy to hear you're ready. Let me hook you up with Gretchen," he said, and I could hear the smile on his face. "The two of you can get started. From my conversations with others, they're finding this to be a rewarding ministry."

Chapter 4: Pets Are Working Saints

Gretchen had been a member of the church for many years when she and the pastor initiated the PAWS ministry at Wesley. My understanding is this was a ministry somewhere in the Methodist Church, and the church provided a guide to jump-start the ministry at a local level. By the time Miss Tucker and I got started, there were about a dozen teams already active with PAWS.

Therapy dog programs operate today that serve as a ministry similar to PAWS. A wonderful example is Canines for Christ. It's an international therapy dog program, started in 2007 by Chaplain Larry Randolph. They have a beautiful website, with stories and faith statements that explain the goal of therapy dog work as a ministry to share the love of Christ with those in need.[5] Very similar to our PAWS program over twenty years ago!

Gretchen had a solid background in dog training. Between the pastor's exuberance and her skills, they were a ready-made team. Tucker was now about five years old, and I felt she was ready, based on the qualifications Gretchen and I'd discussed.

Gretchen called me. "Let's meet at the church and we can do the evaluation there. Tell me again about yours and Tucker's background."

"We've only completed one dog class. We do well with sit, stay and come. But not so good walking in a heel position. But she loves people and is quite calm when she comes up to someone she's not met. And she never jumps," I assured Gretchen.

We met at the church the next day.

"You and Tucker walk around, and I'll watch to see how she listens to you. Ask her to sit and stay. When she's more comfortable with being here and doing all this, I'll see how she does with me petting her," Gretchen instructed us. I thought, *We're good with all this; we run into people all the time on our daily walks and she loves when someone stops to pet her.*

Gretchen worked with me and Tucker for about an hour. Finally, we were accepted and became official PAWS ministers. After we passed our evaluation, Gretchen and her dog Rosy showed us how to function as a PAWS team. One of the organizations Gretchen wanted us to visit was The Baby Fold, a residential home for children with emotional and behavioral challenges. After Rosy and Gretchen showed us how to work at that location, Tucker and I began our PAWS ministry.

A few short years later, Gretchen died from breast cancer. I was beside myself. *How, God, can it be that another beautiful young woman has gone to heaven well before her time?* I was blessed to have had her as a friend and mentor for nearly ten years. Without Gretchen, and the work she did with PAWS, this book would never have been written. Nor would I have experienced the joy of working with the PAWS ministry or Karing Partners, the therapy dog program I created years later at the hospital.

The PAWS ministry was quite active at the time Gretchen passed away. By this time, Pastor Hayes had been sent to another church. But it turned out that the new pastor, Pastor Hoffman, was equally supportive of the PAWS ministry. A few weeks after Gretchen's funeral, he called me.

"I know you and Gretchen were close," he said. "I also know how important the PAWS ministry is to you. I wonder if you'd consider taking over the PAWS ministry here at the church."

I agreed that I loved the ministry. Yes, I loved taking Tucker to be with the kids where we had so much fun, and I loved seeing the kids enjoy the dog. Yes, I'd taken some dog training classes and had even helped Gretchen with some of her training. But there was no way I was capable of teaching dog training classes for the PAWS program!

"I just don't know if I can do this," I told him with great apprehension. "I have zero experience teaching a dog class. I'm still so new at this; I just don't think I'm the person for taking on this task."

He went on to assure me I could do it, and he offered to help in any way possible. In fact, he was thinking of bringing his dog to be a PAWS minister. That put me on the spot. *Really?* I thought. *Just how do I get into these situations?* How could I say no if the pastor was going to bring his dog to be a PAWS minister? I'm not good at saying no, so I simply replied, "Let me think about it."

This time I do recall saying a prayer and asking for direction, since this responsibility was clearly more than I felt ready to tackle! I heard a voice tell me, "Get someone to help you." *Gee,* I thought, *what a grand idea!*

I immediately contacted the local Humane Society to see if they knew of anyone who might help me. They gave me the name of a lady who ran a local dog kennel. Turns out she had experience with a variety of dog breeds through her business and also had experience with dog training.

"Hi, Laurie," I said tentatively when I called her and introduced myself. "I was given your name to see if you might be able to help me with some dog training at my church." I went on to explain our PAWS program.

"Sure, I can help you with that," she said with little hesitation. "I'll get you some dates that work for me and I'll let you set everything up."

"Can you tell me what you might charge for your services?" I asked. I figured this would be the cut-off point. There was no money set aside for this ministry.

"Well, since this is a ministry for your church, I won't charge you for the classes. I've been teaching these classes for more years than I can count. You take charge of getting the participants, handling whatever issues your church needs to address, and I'll just come and teach."

With eagerness in my voice, I called Pastor Hoffman. "I can't believe this, but I found a trainer, and she's willing to teach the class and she is not charging us anything! The format of the class she's going to teach is a Canine Good Citizen class, which I've not heard of. I'll do some checking and see what it is but it sounds like she's ready." Here I am setting up a class for which I knew nothing about! Just what did I think I was doing?

Our goal was to have the first class offered only to church members. I placed a notice in the bulletin, and within three weeks, we had all eight of our spots filled. Laurie had given me instructions about dog health and dog safety she wanted in place. We were going to have eight likely-untrained dogs in the small training space that the church was providing. The choir room, where we held the classes, had a tiled floor in case of any possible "accidents." I was the communication link with the owners for dates and times, doggie behavior expectations and doggie health requirements. I was also charged with moving the chairs used for choir practice out of the way for our class and back in place after class. It was a bit of work but well worth it.

Class participants were encouraged to come a bit early to review the dog health requirements she'd requested. It was also a good time to check out the dog's basic temperament.

When everyone was present, I did introductions and said a prayer. I figured I needed a prayer and assumed the others did too. I prayed for people patience as well as doggie patience. I also prayed for Laurie's patience, but she was cool and calm. Apparently, having worked with dogs most of her life, she had realistic expectations of what behaviors she was going to encounter with a bunch of untrained people and untrained dogs.

We usually started each class with all of the spots filled. Occasionally a few would drop out when they found the commitment was more than they were willing or able to devote to this endeavor. Over the years, more than half of the participants stuck it out and became PAWS ministers. Most of them made visits to nursing homes and similar locations after their graduation.

I remember Carolyn and her well-behaved terrier. She was dedicated to classes and completed the training because her goal was for her and her doggie to have credentials as PAWS ministers so they could visit her mother in the nursing home. She told me years later that visiting with her little terrier was one of the greatest gifts she'd given her mom. Her mother loved the little terrier. The dog would sit on her bed for hours. The joy Carolyn experienced letting the little dog interact with others as they entered and left the nursing home was simply icing on the cake.

PAWS was very important to me, and it still holds a special place in my heart. Not only did I find myself on a path to healing my heart, but to think I could do such wonderful work and be with my dog at the same time, well, miracles do happen! I worked as a PAWS minister for nearly twenty years with all three of my dogs, Tucker, and later, Max and Sadie. Tucker is special: she is the only one of my therapy dogs that Karen knew, and she is the one who helped me start this journey.

Paws for Reflection

God uses ordinary people to do extraordinary things. Consider Moses who many times told God he was not up to God's plan—that he was not the capable person God thought he was. But with God's strength and provision, Moses accomplished great things. God often uses our feelings of inferiority or lack of skills for the purpose of helping others. 1 Peter 5:10 tells us that "the God of all grace, who called you to his eternal glory in Christ, after you have suffered a little while, will himself restore you and make you strong, firm and steadfast."

Does God sometimes ask the impossible? And do his requests feel burdensome? Jesus told his followers, "With man this is impossible, but with God all things are possible" (Matthew 19:26). A burden is the load of responsibility that we carry. God offers to carry the burdens with us. God asks the impossible so that we know how much we need his direction and support.

One of the scriptures I prayed in my PAWS classes was "The Lord does not look at the things people look at. People look at the outward appearance, but the Lord looks at the heart" (1 Samuel 16:7). I hoped to encourage class participants to be patient with training for this ministry; nevertheless, the training sometimes felt impossible! It was tiring and our patience often wore thin. We loved our doggies but sometimes they did not want to do what we asked of them. I reminded them that Galatians 6:9–10 says, "Let us not become weary in doing good, for at the proper time we will reap a harvest if we do not give up. Therefore, as we have opportunity, let us do good to all people, especially to those who belong to the family of believers."

Have you felt a nudge to do the impossible? To take up a cause for others in a way that might be new to you? Imagine something you do in your pastime that might grow into doing something wonderful. If it feels impossible, take it to the Lord; we know that with God all things are possible.

Gail with Sadie (left) and Sally with Oreo (right) at our PAWS graduation

Chapter 5: PAWS Stories

Over the years, a few special people stand out in my PAWS work. Sally and Ken came to the very first PAWS class with Gizmo, then years later brought Bailey and Oreo to be PAWS dogs. Then there was Judy and Doug, another set of repeat participants who also started in the very first class. They brought Kaia and Kyrie and then years later brought Zeni and Zeta. Connie and Zoey were particularly special: Zoey is blind, and Connie was committed to doing PAWS ministry with her. Then there was Marcia who was part of both PAWS and Karing Partners and who was instrumental in me getting my second therapy dog.

Sally and Ken were longtime members of the church and the community. They knew many of the residents at the assisted living/nursing home where PAWS routinely visited. In the later years, when Gizmo and Tucker were in doggie heaven, Ken and Sally and I often worked together at the nursing home.

The residents loved it when Max and little Bailey and Oreo arrived for their visits. They would often remember us from prior visits and were always excited to see us. They told us how cute the dogs looked as they walked the halls together, often with matching scarves and similar coloring. Seeing twenty-pound Bailey or Oreo walk briskly along next to eighty-five-pound Max was quite a sight to see!

We'd meet in the parking lot and let the dogs do their potty. Then we'd walk to the lobby where we'd leave our coats and put a plan together. Sally knew a few of the residents since she'd lived and worked in town all her life. One lady in particular was a good friend Sally had worked with, and we always made a point to visit her.

Sometimes Sally asked if we could visit her friend first. She had worked with this lady and kept in touch with her. "I talked with Laverne the other day and she's excited about our coming to visit. So if you're okay with it, I'd like to start by seeing Laverne first and spend some extra time with her. The dogs seem to have a bit more energy in the early part of our visits and she'd like that."

Often Ken, Sally's husband, would join us too. Ken used a motorized scooter to get around, and he'd ride his scooter along the hallways and interact with the dogs and residents. I always liked when Ken joined us for the visits. Oreo, especially, liked it when Ken was there. Sometimes Oreo would sit on Ken's lap and ride around in the scooter. The residents chuckled seeing Oreo being driven along like a king.

Ken was with us that day, and he directed us to Laverne's room. When Laverne saw Ken, she perked up and said, "Hi. Are the doggies here too?" This was a frequent question for us when we visited and we humans entered the room first. *Really, you came without the dogs? Who wants to just visit with the human? People want to see the dogs!*

"Yes, the dogs are here too," Ken said. He drove his scooter into the room so that Sally and I and the dogs could get in.

"Hi, Oreo and Bailey! Hi, Max!" Sally and I made sure the dogs got up close and personal with Laverne, one on each side of her so she could talk while petting them. At Laverne's request, Sally would place one of her dogs on Laverne's lap. That was the usual routine. All the while we were talking to and visiting with Laverne, she'd pet the dogs. Most of her eye contact was with the dogs as if saying to them, "You agree with me, right?"

It was uplifting to watch how the residents and the dogs interacted. We'd chuckle when the residents and visitors would go on and on petting and talking to the dogs, and then later, as if an afterthought, talk to us humans. They'd talk as if the dogs could understand every word they said. Of course, the dogs loved this special attention, with tails constantly wagging and trying to get closer and closer.

We eventually visited other residents as we walked around the facility. One of our favorite stops was the dining room, which was converted into a movie room after hours. Two ladies in particular stand out in my memory. They just loved Oreo, Bailey and Max. They'd see us walk in and their faces would light up with big smiles. They'd start talking to the dogs as we walked up to them; for Max that meant "Hurry up." We'd make our rounds in the movie area and then move on. Afterward, we'd walk the halls and knock on doors and ask if the resident wanted to see the "special visitors." Sometimes the staff would ask us to make a special effort to stop and see someone they felt would benefit from our presence.

Doug and Judy were one of the other PAWS teams that visited The Baby Fold, along with me and Tucker. Because they brought two dogs for training, they trained with one dog one year and then returned the following year to complete training with the other. That first year they brought Kaia and came the next year with Kyrie. Doug and Judy were determined to complete the training with their young and very active dogs and pass the test to be part of this ministry.

Because of the activity level of the dogs and since there were two of them working together, we'd decided The Baby Fold was most appropriate for them. Judy also had a background as a clinical psychologist, which made her a perfect fit for that location. The kids benefited from everything Doug and Judy brought with them: their love, their commitment, their ability to understand what the kids needed at the moment as well as two high-energy dogs.

The kids quickly figured out when the PAWS dogs were coming to visit and which dogs were coming. They'd be on their best behavior the day the dogs were scheduled to visit since they could only play if they behaved well that day. Bad behavior, no visit with the dogs. Good behavior, visit with the dogs!

Cindy, the supervisor at The Baby Fold we worked with when visiting there, told me a story that involved a number of us. It's about a little girl I'll call Savannah who was afraid of dogs.

"She was scared, but she wanted so badly to see the dogs and play with them," Cindy explained. "So the counselors and I decided to work with her."

"For a few months when you and Max and Doug and Judy would visit, I'd make arrangements for a counselor to come with Savannah while I worked with the other kids like I usually did. But Savannah and the counselor didn't come in, they just watched through the window."

Cindy went on to describe their strategy. "It was such a wonderful opportunity to help build her confidence, we couldn't pass it up. One day Savannah said she wanted to go inside, but not to touch with or play with the dogs, just to watch a bit closer."

After watching the kids and dogs play and interact safely for several months, Savannah finally felt she was ready to touch and personally interact with the dogs. It happened during a visit with Doug and Judy. With Doug and Judy's patience, Judy's special skills as a counselor, and Kaia's special gift of understanding the gentle demeanor this child needed, Savannah finally touched and gently pet Kaia. What an accomplishment! From that point on, whenever the PAWS dogs would visit, Savannah was a regular visitor. Cindy and the other counselors were thrilled at Savannah's accomplishment; they made sure she visited with the dogs as often as possible. It was humbling and exciting to think the PAWS dogs were in some way responsible for making such a positive difference in one little girl's life.

Shortly after, Doug died very unexpectedly while he was on a mission trip. Judy took a break from PAWS, and I didn't see Judy again for many years—until she joined PAWS again many years later.

Another very special PAWS dog was Zoey, a spunky little white Maltese. Connie, another long-standing member of the church, rescued Zoey when she was about a year old. Shortly after Connie rescued her, Zoey began to have problems with her eyes. Sadly Zoey was diagnosed with severe glaucoma, and both of Zoey's eyes needed to be removed. Connie noticed that losing her sight didn't seem to slow Zoey down. When Zoey had fully recovered, Connie called and asked me if I thought Zoey might be able to become a PAWS dog.

Oh boy, this stumped me. By this time, Laurie was no longer teaching the PAWS classes and I had reluctantly taken them on myself. I'd only been teaching the classes a few years and now wondered to myself, *How am I, a very novice dog trainer, going to teach a lady with a blind dog?* I barely felt confident with my teaching, and here I was being asked to do this. Well, as we all know, God has a way of turning the impossible into possible.

"Connie," I said, sounding more confident than I felt, "if you're willing to work with me on this, I'm willing to try. I've only been teaching the PAWS classes for two years and I'm not an expert by any means. But I'm willing to try."

I began researching how to train and work with a blind dog. I read about using sounds like bells on your ankle to let them know your location, using favorite foods in your hand or on a stick for a short dog, and other creative ways to get the dog's attention. It would take a lot of patience for both of us to make this work. We put our heads together on what she thought she could manage and away we went.

There were six dogs in class that year. I felt it was important to get everyone's buy-in to work with Zoey since it was going to take a bit more time and patience than usual, so I got everyone's agreement before we started class. A few class participants that year were repeats with their new dogs, and they were gracious and agreed wholeheartedly. Later, two of the six class participants dropped out before the class was completed, so it ended up working well. We all had lots of time to devote to Connie and Zoey. It was a group on a mission for success!

Because of Connie and Zoey's hard work and the smaller class with seasoned participants, Zoey attained her PAWS diploma and her Canine Good Citizen certificate. I was so moved by Connie and Zoey's efforts that I often made a special attempt to visit with them when they went to work at the nursing home. I was in awe of what they'd accomplished.

What a loving and wonderful ministry this was to both those who provided and those who received the visits. Charles Dickens once said, "No one is useless in this world who lightens the burden of it for anyone else."[6] I think we did that with our doggie work, even if for a moment. I was never quite sure who enjoyed it the most, the giver or the receiver. I continued my work with PAWS as I pursued other activities with dogs, moving into official therapy dog work and working as a therapy dog evaluator. Throughout it all, I hoped Karen was pleased with what I was doing!

Paws for Reflection

As we seek the path that God would have us take, we're reminded God never promised us life would be without its problems. "I have told you these things, so that in me you may have peace. In this world you will have trouble" (John 16:33). But in this same verse, he reminds us he is here to offer us his peace, for the verse ends with "But take heart! I have overcome the world." Familiar biblical heroes such as Moses and David are excellent examples of people who experienced fear and lacked faith in their own strength to complete a task. Moses lacked confidence in his ability to lead and speak publicly. Yet Moses took his concerns to the

Lord, and we read how Moses was later able to speak with the Egyptian pharaoh time and time again and led the Israelites to safety through the Red Sea. And David, throughout the Psalms, prayerfully directs his concerns to God, seeking answers to his many questions, pleading for God to listen to him, and asking God for God's favors and not God's anger.

"Be strong and courageous. Do not be terrified . . . for the Lord your God goes with you; he will never leave nor forsake you" (Deuteronomy 31:6). Often, we are set in our own direction in life when circumstances or other obstacles block our way. Could it be that the pathway we set for ourselves is not what God wants for us? Is it possible he has plans for us that we are unable to discern at the moment? Or could it be that we simply need to be reminded to go to God with our concerns and our hopes and ask for his strength to guide and direct us?

Our PAWS work was not hard, but we went into it without a roadmap or experience. With the Lord's help, we persevered in the direction in which we felt led. Do you have an urge or a feeling of being led to do something in which you lack the skills? Consider praying for strength to move toward that task knowing God will walk that walk with you.

A visit at The Baby Fold

Chapter 6: Miss Tucker

David and I were living in Chicago in 1993 when Tucker came into our lives. We moved shortly afterward to an apartment in Bloomington, Illinois, while we built our home. Since we did not have a yard, Tucker and I went on lots and lots of walks. She loved to walk and would go for miles.

When we finally moved into our home in the countryside near El Paso, Illinois, there was an area nearby on a golf course where we'd walk many miles on the paved trails. There were creeks along the paths and I discovered Tucker loved to swim. Almost every day when we went for a walk, Tucker would go for a swim and then would get a hose-off before we went into the house. In cold weather when the creek water was still open, Tucker would swim and icicles formed on her underside as we walked home. She'd become aware of the icicles and look at me as if to say, "Get these things off me," but it never deterred her from swimming the next day! She never needed a leash when we walked, never left my side and never chased anything. She just wanted to walk and swim. When we visited my mom who lived in the city and she needed a leash, Tucker was quite perturbed by such necessities!

When Tucker and I became PAWS ministers, the PAWS ministry was active in a variety of locations in the community. Gretchen had selected The Baby Fold for us to visit. She had developed a plan with Cindy, the supervisor at The Baby Fold, and after Tucker and I completed our shared visits with Rosy and Gretchen, I worked directly with Cindy to set up our work at The Baby Fold.

Our routine was to visit The Baby Fold once a month. My role was to supervise Tucker's interaction with the children, usually two kids at a time. Tucker loved the active children and was able to keep up with their high level of activity. The kids had to earn "behavior points" to be able to play with the PAWS dogs, and sadly, sometimes they lost their behavior points, and we had to cancel our visit.

Cindy would select two kids and bring them to the gymnasium or the large skating room where we'd interact with the kids. On a nice summer day, we'd be outside in the large fenced-in playground. Usually, another counselor would come with Cindy to supervise the other child. Cindy would instruct the kids on how they could interact with the dogs.

When they arrived, Cindy would first introduce us to the kids. "Gail, this is Jason and Aaron. Jason and Aaron, can you say hi to Gail and Tucker? Tucker's here to play with you for about twenty minutes. You'll each get some time with Tucker, but just one at a time."

I'd say hello and ask Tucker to shake their hands. The kids got a kick out of that. Cindy would pick one child to be the first to play with Tucker. "You must listen to Ms. Gail and do what she tells you. She'll be making sure Tucker plays safely with you." The kids learned skills of sharing as they went back and forth during their time with the dog. It was inspiring to see one kid, who Cindy said never exhibited such generous behavior in the residence or at school, offer to share the leash and they'd walk together with Tucker. There were numerous times when the kids worked with each other to set up five-minute play-time intervals with Tucker. Most of the time, they honored their agreement and would readily give Tucker to the other child at the agreed-upon time. The kids were learning skills they might not have had an opportunity to learn in any other setting.

Many children we worked with had some evidence of ADHD (attention deficit hyperactivity disorder) and were challenged when attempting to relate to people. There's a large body of evidence that shows the use and presence of dogs helps these children learn how to relate better. The University of California, Irvine in Orange County, CA, posted articles about the usefulness of therapy dogs for children with ADHD. Their findings support what we saw happen right in front of our eyes: Therapy dogs can be beneficial for children, especially challenged kids, in a supervised setting.[7]

Cindy told me she'd select the kids for visits that had been well behaved or sometimes she'd select them based on a particular need she and the other counselors identified. They felt a few minutes with the dogs could be therapeutically beneficial. The kids were learning to follow directions as well as interact with a safe dog. A safe encounter with a dog was something many of them had no prior experience with. The kids would walk and run with Tucker, pet her and brush her. Cindy and I watched to make sure the kids were interacting as they'd been instructed.

During our PAWS visits, Tucker was always on a leash. I'd give the leash to the kids and they'd run with her. Since I had to supervise, I ran right alongside them. It was a great time to talk with the kids about good dog interaction with a dog that was not dangerous. Tucker was able to show them how to touch and make good contact with a safe dog. The kids would tell stories of dogs they'd been around, that they'd been afraid of, or stories of friends with vicious dogs and dog bites and so on. It was a joy to see them play safely and love on Tucker. It was evident Tucker loved being with them as she was always eager to meet the next batch of kids, tail wagging constantly, and never seemed to tire of being active with the kids. She was incredibly tolerant of their quick movements and the number of kids she interacted with each visit. Sometimes the kids would give Tucker multiple commands all at one time and she'd look at me as if to ask, "What do I do now?"

Cindy was a strong supporter of the PAWS visits. "The kids are having fun, yes. But they're also learning how to safely *be* with a big dog. They're learning there are gentle dogs that provide love and love them back. And I'm so grateful to observe the kids and dogs together because I see a soft side of these tough kids I don't see at other times. The dogs bring that out in them. We often see only the problems with the kids. I wish all the counselors could see this side of the kids."

Each pair of children had downtime with Tucker. This is when we'd ask the kids to slow down and let Tucker rest. I taught them how to ask Tucker to sit or lay down. They'd lay down next to her and love on her. Lots of kisses and hugs and special whispers I'd sometimes see. Shared Tucker-time was when kids would be together with Tucker in quiet time. Talking, petting and brushing were the activities of this quiet time. It was a joy to see these troubled kids be in a safe and special place for just a few minutes, to find a shared activity where they would tolerate each other and find they had something in common.

One night when we arrived, I was told an official visitor was there. The staff working with the kids had told the visitor of our PAWS adventures. She asked if she could speak with me before we started our visit. "Sure thing," I said.

"I've heard stories of using therapy dogs with children in this type of setting, but I've never seen it for myself. Can you tell me about it?" she asked.

"This is an informal activity; it's a ministry through our church," I explained. "We bring the dogs to visit with kids who've earned good behavior points. A few of us have been doing this long enough that we see the benefits and how the kids enjoy it. I think the dogs like it too! Tucker knows where we're going when we come for PAWS, and we have a special routine to get ready to visit: special leash and collar and I tell her we are going to see the kids. She gets quite excited."

When this person first heard of the PAWS visits, she was skeptical. But as the stories went on and the kids talked about how they enjoyed our visits and shared Tucker's photos and other things that were evidence of our visits, she became interested.

"Love for these kids can be demonstrated in a variety of ways, and this is just one way we're doing that," I explained to her. I described our training process for the dogs as well as for the people who visited the children. She decided to stay and watch our PAWS ministry in action.

We went about our routine of two kids visiting at a time, my supervision of Tucker with one child and the facility's supervision of the other child. We ran and brushed and played and had quiet petting time as we always did. As usual, the kids were excited and gave Miss Tucker three and four commands at a time, and Tucker looked at me with her standard "What do I do now?" look. A pretty routine visit as far as I was concerned.

Afterward, she thanked me for letting her observe. She told me she saw gentle and kind and loving behaviors from the children that she had not seen or thought likely based on their behavioral history. I shared some of the stories from those of us who had watched the kids work with our PAWS dogs, even in the limited time we were able to spend with them, and knew something special was taking place. I was grateful for the opportunity to demonstrate our ministry in action that day.

One of Tucker's favorite things to do was to "take it." Typical of many retrievers, she loved carrying things in her mouth. We made a special attempt at Christmas to give each child a card with a different photo of Tucker and a McDonald's gift certificate. Tucker's special gift to the kids was to "take it" (our gift) to each child as part of their visit that evening. We made sure we had extra cards for the kids who couldn't make it to PAWS the night we visited. We discovered later the kids would often swap their photos and hang them on their bulletin board.

Cindy told me about a past resident she'd recently heard from. The child wrote a note to Cindy and thanked her for all the good things they had experienced at The Baby Fold. One of those good things was the PAWS dogs.

Miss Tucker got sick one evening, just after Thanksgiving. We took her to the local emergency veterinary clinic where they inserted a tube into her stomach. They said she had something called gastric dilatation-volvulus (GDV), a condition where the stomach "flips" when it fills with gas, food or fluid. When the tube did not help, they sent us to the university clinic. The university clinic said there was nothing they could do when we got her there, it was too late. I remember thinking: *How can this be?* Tucker was only eight years old. She was active and healthy, and we had work to do!

They placed us in a quiet room, just me, David and Miss Tucker. They were very kind. We lay on the floor with her, touched her and talked to her as they administered the medication; first to sedate her, then the medication that stopped her heart. My heart was broken.

I made the difficult call to The Baby Fold and told them Tucker would not be back. A few weeks later, Cindy called and asked me to come by as the kids had something for me. They had each made me a sympathy card, and together they made a large poster with their illustrated version of Tucker as a therapy dog and signed all of their names. They said I could come back and visit, even though I did not have a dog. I still have that poster nearly twenty-five years later.

Paws for Reflection

It is hard to believe that God chose me, insignificant me, to do something as good as PAWS. I am reminded that God gives each of us unique gifts. "We have different gifts, according to the grace given to each of us. If your gift is prophesying, then prophesy in accordance with your faith; if it is serving, then serve; if it is teaching, then teach; if it is to encourage, then give encouragement; if it is giving then give generously; if it is to lead, do it diligently; if it is to show mercy, do it cheerfully" (Romans 12:6–8). It is up to us to identify and then find a way to use the gifts he gives us. 1 Peter 4:10 boldly tells us that "Each of you should use whatever gift you have received to serve others, as faithful stewards of God's grace in its various forms."

Once we find a place in which to use the gifts we have been given, we may ask, *Where is God taking me? What does he want me to do with this?* If we let him, he can take us to amazing places, places full of possibilities we might never have imagined. Proverbs 3:5–6 says it best: "Trust in the Lord with all your heart and lean not on your own understanding; in all your ways submit to him, and he will make your paths straight."

God wants the best for us. He wants us to find joy and love in our lives here on Earth. What brings you joy? Have you discovered or prayed about the gifts God has given you? How might you use the gifts he has given you for the work of his kingdom? Pray and meditate; talk with trusted people in your life to find out what special gifts you have been given. Employ those gifts for sharing with others.

Gail with Max

Chapter 7: Becoming a Therapy Dog

After losing Tucker in 2003, we decided we'd get another dog. David supported me in the PAWS work I was doing and understood it was something I felt strongly about. As we talked about how to go about this, I knew one thing for sure: We were going to do whatever it took to become a certified therapy dog team!

We took a few months and mulled the decision over carefully. Were we going to get another puppy? If we got a puppy, I could start training the dog right away. But what about an older dog? What about a rescue? There were pros and cons to both. After much deliberation, we decided our dog would be a rescue, ideally not a puppy but maybe two or three years old.

But how were we going to do this? I talked to people, looked online and visited the local rescues. I decided to start with the Humane Society.

I went to the Humane Society mid-morning on a Saturday. I thought I'd complete the application and see how it went. I was told the application was a lengthy process and would take a few days to approve. The questionnaire was four pages long and asked me just about everything except my height and weight! Since we'd already had a dog, I was able to answer most questions without much effort.

One element of the required information was a reference. I put down the number for the vet we'd worked with for Tucker and completed the application. Before I left to go home, I called the vet's office to let them know a call might be coming. It was already 11:00 a.m. and I knew they closed at 11:30 a.m. The Humane Society also closed at noon that day so figured I'd be all set for next week when things would start to happen. I was excited on the drive home thinking about the possibilities of a new dog!

Just as I entered the house, the phone was ringing. It was the vet's office. Kathy the receptionist was talking so fast, I could hardly understand her. "I just got a call from the Humane Society, and they told me you filled out an application. They wanted to know if we'd consider you an acceptable dog owner. I told them all about the PAWS thing you're involved in and told them *yes,* they need to give you any dog you wanted!"

I was laughing because she talked so fast. I replied, "Thanks, Kathy, I'm pretty excited. They didn't want to show me any dogs because they have to review the application and get recommendations first. I'm shocked she called you already."

"I know losing Tucker was hard on both of you. We think you'd be great with any dog. Just call and let us know when you get your new doggie and we'll get you in right away."

As soon as I hung up, the phone rang again. I answered immediately.

"Hi. This is the Humane Society. We wanted to let you know that you've been approved to adopt a dog. We noticed you had a golden retriever in the past and your veterinarian said you'd be a good fit for one of our dogs," the person on the other end of the phone said. *That was fast,* I thought.

"Yes, we lost our goldie a few months ago, but we're ready to adopt. We're willing to talk about any of the dogs you have right now." I still assumed we were talking about next week or the following week. "If it matters in any way, I want you to know we're planning to do therapy dog work with the dog we get. So that will be one of our deciding factors. But we're open to whatever dogs you have."

"Believe it or not," she went on, "we have a nice male golden retriever in the back that we've kept for about eight weeks attempting to locate his owners. He was found wandering the streets and was turned in as a stray. We don't have any other background on him, but he seems to like people. With your background with goldens, we thought you might like to see him."

I knew their office was now closed. And since I was getting ready to go out of town to visit my mom, I said, "I'd love to see him. How about if I come in on Monday?"

The person on the other end of the phone hesitated a moment. "He'll be going up for public adoption on Monday. If you'd like to see him today, we'll be happy to have you come back right now if you can get here right away."

"I'll be there in twenty minutes," I said as I hurried out the door and got into my car. *What am I thinking*, I thought? *David is working today and can't be part of this decision, so what should I do?*

I hustled back into town and went to the back entrance of the building. Someone was waiting to meet me. We went into the large area toward the back where there were many kennels and walked to the kennel where Boomer was. The folks at the Humane Society had named him, just as they name all the animals in their care. Someone thought "Boomer" would work. But I knew right away that "Boomer" just wouldn't work for a therapy dog.

He was a small male, weighing only fifty-five pounds. And he was so gentle. When we got near his kennel, he was a bundle of excitement. Wiggles, tail wags and doggie whimpers. He came out of his kennel and immediately rolled on his back. He was so excited to get tummy rubs! I knew that was a good sign; a dog that rolls over in a submissive position upon first greeting is not usually aggressive. For our therapy dog work, I was looking for a more laid-back dog, so it was love at first sight.

I was ready to take him home then and there. But I still had to talk to David and make sure he was okay with this decision. What's more, I'd promised my mom I'd come to see her for the weekend. As I spoke with the lady at the Humane Society, she suggested we might want to take him to the vet before we took him home, just to get a good checkup from our vet. Simply too many reasons why I could not take him right then and there. I was sad, but I needed to wait till Monday to come back and get him. Would they be willing to keep him till Monday? They agreed.

I went home and called David right away. We both agreed the dog sounded like a good fit for us, but we'd wait to bring him home on Monday. I thought spending some time with my mom would be a good way to plan for the adoption, considering her background with so many dogs. And I knew she'd love to be in on the discussion.

So off I went to Oshkosh. She was a good sounding board, and we talked all weekend. She was elated that we were getting another dog, but she had some good questions for us to consider.

"What do you know about him?" she inquired.

"Not much," I replied. "Only that he was found on the streets in town. They didn't tell me if someone turned him in or if they sort of captured him. Just said he was a stray. They think he was wandering for quite a while. Apparently, he was quite thin when he first showed up. They said he's gained weight while he's been with them, but I don't know, he sure is skinny now, I can't imagine what he weighed when he was brought in."

"What are you going to do if he doesn't work out? He's a big dog and you don't know his personality or anything." She was concerned about his history and possibly being abused. Were we ready to tackle that issue?

"I think his turning tummy-up when we met him tells me a good bit about his personality. And he's a goldie—so likely he is going to have a pretty good disposition." We discussed more, and she gave me some possible outcomes to consider. Mom and I went back and forth on names and we decided Max was a strong and pleasant name that would work well for a therapy dog. Since David and I had pretty much decided to go forward with the adoption, after taking with my mom I was ready to go back and get Max.

I was at the Humane Society first thing Monday morning. I completed the adoption papers and brought up some of the concerns we'd contemplated over the weekend. They assured me if things didn't work out, we could bring him back. That sounded awful, and I hoped it would not be an option we'd need to consider. In my heart, though, I knew I'd never be able to take him back since I was already in love. But it was nice to have the assurance.

I took him directly to the vet. Dr. Bleem thoroughly checked him over. The first thing he told me was Max was considerably underweight. I thought Max was a bit thin, but Dr. Bleem said he was grossly underweight at fifty-five pounds. A combination of his roaming around town, an ear infection and an infection from him being neutered all combined to make him quite emaciated. They got him fixed up, they bathed him, and we brought him home.

We were going to be good dog parents and planned to keep Max kenneled till we were confident he was house broken and a bit more familiar with being in his new home. Max had other plans. There was no way he was going to be kept in a kennel. I guess eight weeks in the kennel at the Humane Society was simply too much for this wandering dog. Against our better judgment, we left him to run free in the house while we worked during the day. He proved to be a good boy, and never got into any trouble. And what a good appetite he had! Max eventually peaked out at eighty-five pounds! We dealt with chronic ear infections that required twice-daily treatments, but our Mellow Max gently tolerated those treatments for the rest of his life.

We never did figure out where Max came from and could only imagine where he'd been. For instance, we were told that Max was only one or two years old, yet his teeth were worn down so low they were worse than our present twelve-year-old dog's teeth. He loved to hold rocks in his mouth, but he never chewed or swallowed them. And he did not know how to play! He simply refused to play tug of war. When we tried to play fetch with him, he'd slowly run to the ball. But when he got there, he'd stop and sit. Then he'd look at us like, "What do I do now?" and he just sat there. We gave up on fetch.

When we put him on a leash, he would walk slowly and gently. We walked the same paths I used to walk with Tucker, near woods and streams. A golden retriever should love to swim, right? Max would have none of it. Water is for fish, and he decided he was no fish. He tolerated his baths like he tolerated everything else with his gentle demeanor, but no way was he going swimming. Initially, he was afraid of cars and traffic and walking over bridges, and we attributed that to his being on the streets. But he loved people. Whenever he was approached, he was welcoming and gentle. So we figured he'd forgiven whoever or whatever was responsible for him becoming a stray. We came to call him Mellow Max.

We were thrilled that we were able to rescue Max. The Humane Society of the United States (HSUS) has a long history of working with animals needing care. In January 2022, they reported that more than one million cats and dogs each year are euthanized because they're not adopted.[8] While some instances involve animals with health and behavior concerns, the majority simply need to find homes. There are many reasons to consider rescuing a shelter animal: you're saving a life (many have lived in a home and re-adapt well when given the chance), you're fighting puppy mills, you're giving an older animal a second chance, and from personal experience, I believe the animals are truly appreciative!

By this time, in 2002, therapy dogs were becoming more commonplace across the country. We'd planned for Max to eventually become a PAWS dog, like Tucker. So because of Max's gentle and loving personality and my desire to have a certified therapy dog, we decided we'd go full throttle, begin training and scope out opportunities for us to do this work right away. I looked into what we needed to do. I figured the best place to start was obedience classes.

The local dog training center offered beginner, intermediate and advanced dog obedience classes. We started with beginners. We went to the full eight weeks of class. We failed our test. So we went back and took the beginners class over again. This time we passed. Next came the intermediate class. We went to the full eight weeks of class and again failed the first time around. One of us just wasn't getting this! Hmm . . . whenever the trainers asked Max to do his sit, down, stay and come, he did just fine. So guess who really needed the training? It was the same for our advanced class, but this time I anticipated our need to repeat, and I was ready! Training is a good time to bond, and we decided to just enjoy it and keep going. I was no doubt the one who needed the training. Max did everything I asked him to do. I just needed to learn how to ask in a way he could understand.

When we completed the advanced class the second time around, we looked for therapy dog classes. At the time, the local training center did not offer classes to prepare for therapy dog work. I'd read that a Canine Good Citizen (CGC) test was not required but was considered to be good preparation for the therapy dog test. I'd done research years before when Laurie taught the PAWS classes at the church and gave CGC certificates, so I was familiar. I found a training center about forty miles from our home that offered a CGC test to anyone who felt prepared. Considering the remedial education it seemed I needed, I decided the CGC test as a practice would be good for the next step. We signed up for the test.

"Hi. We're Gail and Max here for the CGC test," I informed the lady who was checking us in.

"Are you part of our class? I don't recall you being at our classes," she noted. I was a bit perplexed as I'd not seen anything online indicating we needed to have taken a class.

"No," I replied. "We didn't take your class. I found your information online and signed up. It didn't say we needed to be part of the class first. But we've completed basic, intermediate and advanced obedience classes at another facility," I explained. I didn't tell her that we'd failed each class the first time through. But Max and I had reviewed and practiced the behaviors we'd need to demonstrate, so I tried to be hopeful.

"Okay. You can test. You'll be the last ones tonight, after all the others have tested." She indicated where we were to sit until we were called. I remember having mixed feelings watching all the other teams perform the required activities. I was grateful Max was so relaxed and did not pick up on my anxiety. We were the last called that evening and we passed!

Now we were ready for the next step: taking the therapy dog test. Thank goodness for Google and the internet because there were no testing options or active therapy dog teams in the local community at that time. So, again, I started my research.

Therapy dogs come in all sizes and breeds. The most important characteristic of a therapy dog is its temperament. "A certified therapy dog must be friendly, patient, confident, gentle, and at ease in all situations. Therapy dogs should enjoy human contact and be content to be petted, cuddled, and handled, sometimes clumsily, by unfamiliar people and to enjoy that contact."[9]

All the locations I found for therapy dog testing were well over fifty miles from our home. I wasn't sure this was going to work. I finally found a test about thirty miles from where my mom lived in Wisconsin. I contacted the organization to make sure an interstate test would be acceptable and set us up for the test. We stayed at my mom's the weekend we took the test.

"I'm so nervous about this," I lamented. "A new town, I don't know any of the people there, and what if we don't pass?"

"And what if you do pass?" My mother was the most optimistic person you could ever meet. Nothing deterred her from thinking all would work out well. "There's no reason to think you won't pass. And if you don't pass, you can just come back here and take the test again."

Max and I drove to Fond du Lac to take the test. Just as with our CGC test, the people testing all knew each other. So, again feeling a bit out of place, we stood off to the sideline until we were called. This time I wasn't able to watch the teams that were testing, which was probably a good thing. When it was all said and done, and after all my concerns and worries about not passing, Max did a wonderful job and we passed. Max and Gail: We were an official therapy dog team! Now we just needed to figure out what we were going to do with our newfound opportunity.

Paws for Reflection

Scripture encourages us to rejoice in our blessings and give God thanks for all things good and right. Among those things good and rights are our animals. God created us all. Psalm 50:10–11 says, "For every animal of the forest is mine, and the cattle on a thousand hills. I know every bird in the mountains and the insects in the fields are mine."

God created all animals, including our dogs, for them to be our helpers as well as our companions. St. Francis of Assisi is known for his love of animals and is called the Patron Saint of Animals. He sought out animals and even prayed for them. He had great respect for all life, seeing all creation as his brother and sister in Christ. St. Francis saw God's incredible goodness in the creatures he created.

Is it a good thing to have dogs and other animals in our life? God wants us to find joy in this life. I believe for many of us, our animals bring us the kind of joy that allows and enables us to share the love of God with others.

God asks us to share that love with others. Might it be possible for you to share God's love by sharing your animal, especially your dog, with others? Can you even go one step further and consider your dog becoming a therapy dog? "The King will reply, 'Truly I tell you, whatever you did for one of the least of these brothers and sisters of mine, you did for me'" (Matthew 25:40).

Mellow Max with his favorite toy

Chapter 8: Mellow Max

Max was born to be a therapy dog. We knew nothing about his past except that he was found living on the streets in the city. How could a beautiful, likely full-bred golden retriever end up on the streets? What became evident over time is that he was not abused. He loved attention, loved being with people, and was very mellow. Once he sailed through his obedience classes (I was the one who had to repeat!) and his CGC and therapy dog tests, we were ready to get started.

I contacted Cindy at The Baby Fold. She was thrilled to hear we were ready to begin our PAWS work again, this time with Max who by now had his CGC and therapy dog certificates. Max and I went to see Cindy so she could evaluate his readiness to work with the kids. She loved meeting Max and felt he was more than ready! We got started the next week.

It didn't take long for me to realize there was something different about Max's approach to this work compared to Tucker. Where Tucker loved to be active and run and essentially meet the kids' activity where they gave it, Max was going to do it his way—and it was going to be mellow. When the kids wanted to run, Max wanted to walk. When the kids wanted to sit and pet and brush Max, he was all for it! For the longest time, I shared with Cindy my concerns about the kids not connecting as well with Max, but she assured me it would work out.

What can we learn from our dogs? Little research has been done in this area, but there's wonderful anecdotal information. Cesar Milan, somewhat of a dog psychologist, talks about the need to go beyond our comfort zone and learn how to be calm and assertive at the same time. He gives wonderful examples of where people can learn from dogs. He describes a therapy dog team working with brain-injured children that found the dogs helped the children in many ways including developing motor skills, performing select tasks, touching properly and building confidence.[10]

After six months of working with the kids, Max finally decided he'd pick up the pace a bit. We usually saw three or four sets of kids each evening, with two kids in each session. Each rotation lasted about twenty minutes. We had a short rest period in-between as one set of kids went out and another was brought in. We discovered Max was ready for stepped-up activity for the first round of kids. Then a bit more laid back in the second set. By the third round, we were definitely only walking. If there was a fourth group, we were petting and brushing way more than we were walking. At first, I was concerned that we were not meeting the kids' desires to be active and play. But Cindy assured me this mellow activity was what the kids needed. While Tucker provided an outlet for activity, Max provided a platform for the kids to learn to be calm and settled.

Cindy used Max's approach to pick and choose the right kids for the right session. Some of the kids were in the first group one month and another group the next month. She used the differences in Max's actions and the difference in his behavior at each session throughout the evening as a teachable moment for the kids.

Max brought out the best in the kids. He was ever so patient with every child. He never buckled if the hugs were too tight. Back when Tucker would get multiple commands all at once, like sit, stay and come, she'd look at me for direction. Not Max. When kids did the multiple-commands thing with Max, he decided he would do one of them and that was it. So if the kids started with sit, that was the command he was going to follow. If they were walking with Max and the kids told him to heel, then sit or lie down, he simply kept on walking. The supervisors and I got such a kick out of watching Max. He taught the kids they needed to decide what they wanted because they were only going to be successful once! I was able to be up close and personal with their commands and Max's response since I was always right next to him, watching for his safety as well as the kids'. Toward the end of the evening, he was tired, and he'd look at me with a special look and I knew it was time to stop and go home. Even the kids came to understand Max's control of the sessions, and they knew if they were part of session one, they could be pretty active. But they also knew if it was session four, it was going to be "sit on the floor" and just have quiet time. Over time I came to understand Cindy's assurance that the kids would truly learn from Mellow Max.

Max and I had participated a few times in a reading program with kids at the library in our local community. So we tried a similar activity with the kids at The Baby Fold, thinking a calm activity might help the kids learn it was good to be calm. We made a few attempts. Max was willing, but the kids had experienced more active endeavors with the dogs and they were more interested in the more interactive adventures with the dogs.

Cindy once told me a story. "I'm starting to notice some interesting trends with some of the kids." She chuckled a bit as she shared her analysis with me. "I think they've figured out if they behave the week Max comes to visit, they get to play with him. I notice on the weeks when he does not visit, they tend to misbehave a bit. They know that if they misbehave on the week Max comes, they can't play with him." She gave me a few examples and told me she and the other supervisors had recently noted this pattern. We laughed and talked about how they'd come to figure this out. Inwardly, I beamed with delight.

To think that Max's visits were meaningful to these kids who had such a hard time simply with life was tremendously gratifying. It made me think of driving on a dreary road, on a hot summer day, when the stop for an ice cream cone takes you to a place of momentary bliss. It doesn't change the heat of the day or the rough road, but somehow it adds a new dimension of acceptance and even joy in the rest of the trip.

All the while Max and I were active with PAWS at The Baby Fold, we also made regular visits to the nursing home. We often visited with Sally and Ken and all their dogs; first with Gizmo then later with Bailey and

Oreo. Just as the kids enjoyed seeing Max, the residents and staff at the nursing home enjoyed his visits just as much. It was a joy to see how well Max worked as a PAWS dog in multiple settings. I felt he was created to be a therapy dog. And what he taught me about therapy dog work in return was immeasurable. With the joy we experienced at The Baby Fold, I knew there were more opportunities in our future. I thought back to my time with Karen's Preston and Tanner, what I had watched them do for Karen. How could I take those memories and help move me forward? What would be next?

Paws for Reflection

God is good. He provides for us, loves us and wants the best for us. But he also gives us the freedom to choose to follow his guide, or not. It is the choosing that comes from the heart. Choosing God and his way doesn't mean we're spared from sadness, failures, disease and the like, but having freely chosen to follow his lead, he does promise us joy. The fruit of the Spirit, which is the outcome of our walk with the Lord, is joy and a life of blessings. This is told to us by the apostle Paul in Galatians 5:22–23, "But the fruit of the Spirit is love, joy, peace, forbearance [patience], kindness, goodness, faithfulness, gentleness, and self-control."

I think Max exemplified much of what Paul says to us in this verse. Max's approach to life and to all he met was love, joy, patience, kindness, goodness, gentleness and self-control. Everyone who met Max found him a joy to be around. In multiple obedience classes, he was asked to be the buffer dog between other dogs that did not get along. Max lived by the reminder in Hebrews 13:1–2 to "Keep on loving one another as brothers and sisters. Do not forget to show hospitality to strangers, for by so doing some people have shown hospitality to angels without knowing it." He was Mellow Max in everything he did. He was never in a hurry; he took his time with everything he did. He was truly a great example of who and what we can be when we follow God's teachings.

Look at yourself in the mirror. Think about Max and picture his gentle demeanor. Do you act like Max? Do you display the attributes that Paul talks about in Galatians? If not, think about where you can make changes. Ask God for directions on how to do this. Pray for God's intervention in your life to show the hospitality to others that he requests.

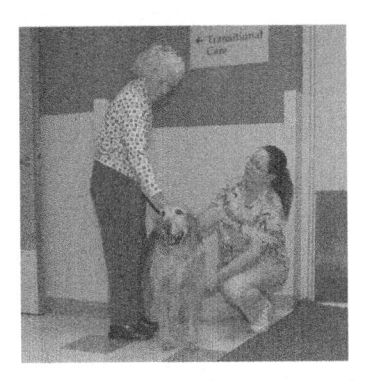

Tammy and Gail with Max outside the hospital unit

Chapter 9: Max Visits

I was having so much fun working with Max and the kids, I decided we were ready to do more. By 2004, therapy dog activities were beginning to blossom all over the United States. I looked at articles, watched TV and talked to anyone I could who might know something about therapy dogs.

At the time, I was working at the hospital as an educator. One of the departments I was responsible for was the hospital's transitional care unit, also called a skilled care or rehabilitation unit. I often interacted with Tammy, the activity director. One of the things she was responsible for was setting up daily activities. In casual conversation one day, she indicated one of the sanctioned activities was animal visits. *Wow, could this be an opportunity dropped right in my lap?* I thought.

I approached Tammy the next day as I walked into the unit. "I did some thinking and wonder if you'd be open to a crazy idea. I've wanted to do something more with Max now that he has the PAWS thing down pat." Tammy had heard me talk about Max plenty of times.

"Okay," she said, looking at me quizzically, "I'm listening."

I explained. "I've been checking out what kinds of things we can do with our therapy dog certificate. You'd mentioned animals as an activity, so I checked the Medicare regulations for skilled care and I see animals are an accepted 'activity' for units like this. Would you be willing to talk about getting Max approved as one of your scheduled activities?"

"Mmm . . . sounds interesting," she said as she mulled it over. "I struggle trying to come up with different activities. This just might work. But we'll have to talk to Marcia [the unit manager] and see what she thinks. We had people from the zoo come a few years back and that went well. But they quit coming. Seems if the zoo critters could come, you guys can surely come!" I reminded her Max had his therapy dog certificate, we had experience with PAWS, and I knew the unit and staff well. We both thought it was worth a try.

We took our request to the department leaders. After a lengthy discussion, a review of Max's credentials and his work history, we got the approval to get started. Tammy took the lead in getting Max on the activity calendar. As the unit educator, I was charged with providing education to the employees. They felt special to be selected as the only unit where we'd be visiting. There was a sense of excitement. The therapy dog associations required me to be a volunteer when doing therapy dog work, so we were transparent about that in our plans and education.

When Max and I arrived for our visits, we'd stop at the nurse's station to announce our presence. Then Tammy or one of the other staff members would visit the patients and ask if they wanted to see the "special visitor." While they were interviewing the residents, Max and I visited with the staff. The employees loved our visits, and Max loved all the attention! Once we received our go-ahead, Max and I started our rounds.

You can imagine the surprise of the patients and visitors when we appeared on the unit. A dog visiting in the hospital! All of this took place in the early days of therapy dog work in hospitals, so this was a big deal in this mid-sized, Midwestern city. But we were met with such enthusiasm! The smiles, the laughter, and even the squeal of children were such joyful experiences. One of my favorite memories is the squeal of young children visiting their grandparents when they saw a big, gentle dog walking down the hallway and visiting with them.

After a while, word was out around the hospital that Max was a regular visitor to the transitional care unit. While I was working in my role as an educator, people would ask me when Max was coming in next. Oftentimes, employees would make a special effort to come to the transitional care unit and visit with Max when we were there.

When others in the main hospital heard about the "dog in the hospital," we had our share of naysayers. We made it a point to be exceedingly careful about cleanliness and behavior protocols.

One day Max and I were visiting in a room. The infectious disease doctor came in. "And just who do we have here?" he asked as he walked over to pet Max. *Oh boy,* I thought. *Here we go, get ready to be asked to leave and not come back.*

"This is Max, he's a therapy dog. We were just here talking and visiting and making everybody happy," I explained, feeling a bit less anxious based on his upbeat demeanor.

"I think this is just wonderful. I'm very much a dog lover." And he went on to talk about his family dogs, all the while petting and looking at Max. The patient was

Chapter 9: Max Visits

smiling and engaged with the doctor in a general dog discussion. I was still somewhat nervous.

"I'm glad to see you doing this work. It's a good service for the hospital to offer to patients who are here for a long time. One of the other hospitals where I work does something similar." Max and I left so he could examine the patient, but we were excited! We knew we'd just knocked down a huge potential roadblock to our efforts!

Were we doing a good thing? The nurses smiled when we visited, and the doctor gave us positive acknowledgment for what we were doing. But what about the patients and their families? Max and I were leaving the unit one day and a lady followed us out. I recognized her as the daughter of one of the patients we'd just visited.

"I can't thank you enough for this work you're doing. My dad has been a patient here for about six weeks, getting his intravenous medication. Today is the first day I've seen a smile on his face. We didn't know if he was going to be able to make it at home because he's been so depressed. But he talked so much today, and it's the first time I've felt any hope that he was going to make it through this ordeal," she said, petting Max the entire time. I guess I had my answer.

Max and I'd been visiting the unit for about a year when one day as we were leaving, a gentleman motioned

117

for us to stop by his car. He was picking up his wife who worked at the hospital. In the backseat, waiting and watching for his mom to come out, was Jake, a little West Highland terrier. Jake and Tom had been watching Max and I exit the hospital several times as he waited for his wife. Tom asked all sorts of questions about what we were doing and how we got started. He asked if he and Jake might get involved. Tom was retired and he said he and Jake needed something to do.

I approached Tammy and we talked about Tom's request. Tom received the okay for Jake to visit, but only if Jake and Max visited together. Jake did not have any credentials, but this was in the early days of therapy dog work, and based on Jake's good manners, his excellent health record, his personality and his love of people, he was given the green light.

Jake and Max got along famously. The staff, patients and visitors loved it when the dogs were there. And apparently, somebody thought we were newsworthy. The hospital's marketing department set up a date with the local newspaper to take photos and interview us about the work we were doing. So Max and Flakey Jake (as he came to be called) had their pictures taken and their story printed in the local newspaper.

We were honored to be in a newspaper article on November 22, 2004. Both Max and Flakey Jake were photographed, and patients and staff were interviewed about the work the dogs were doing. The article told about Max and Flakey Jake making their rounds and how they were bathed and brushed and teeth brushed before their visit. The article talked about how Max, a big dog, and Flakey Jake, a little dog, get along so well. Tammy Puckett, the activity director, said staff members had a special smile when they saw the dogs.[11]

Max and I visited about once or twice a month for nearly six years. By that time, it was fairly common knowledge that dog activity was taking place on the transitional care unit. One day when I was working and making my rounds in the emergency department, I was stopped by one of the nurses.

"I heard you're bringing your dog to the transitional care unit," she said as she approached me with a bit of a lift in her step. "I'm interested in knowing more about what you're doing. I talked to one of the nurses there and she said they love it when you and Max visit."

I told her I appreciated her comments and explained what we were doing. "Max is so gentle and mellow and he was certified as a therapy dog a few years ago. I got a few ideas from things I'd seen on TV about therapy dog visits to hospitals. Then things sort of fell into place here, and we've been visiting ever since. We both love it, and we've not had any problems or complaints."

"Have you considered doing this work here in the main hospital?" she asked. "I have a golden retriever also named Max and I'd love to do some therapy dog work." She said she and her husband had just finished classes. "We took the Canine Good Citizen class and then went on and got Max certified as a therapy dog. I'm so ready and pumped to think about how we can get started. When I heard you were doing this, I wanted to talk to you about how we might get involved."

"Well," I sort of dragged my feet and then told her, "I haven't given much thought to that, Michelle. I'm busy with the transitional care unit, and Max and I are doing therapy dog work with our church. I know this type of thing exists, but I wouldn't have the faintest idea how to get something like that started." I knew hospital-wide therapy dog activity was taking place all over the United States, but I'd been busy, loved what I was doing and truly had not given thought to do more.

Michelle ended with a promise. "If you're willing, I'll help you get this started. We need to do therapy dog work throughout the hospital. Since you and Max have done this successfully with no issues after all these years, now is the time to make it go big! Max and I will work with you, and we can be the first dog teams to visit here in the hospital. I'll do anything you need me to do. Let's make this happen!"

Paws for Reflection

God does good things for us. He gives us food for our tables, families and friends to love, beauty in the world around us, and jobs or hobbies we love. "Now all glory to God, who is able, through his mighty power at work within us, to accomplish infinitely more than we might ask or think ... Glory to him in the church and in Christ Jesus through all generations forever and ever! Amen" (Ephesians 3:20–21 NLT). For those open to his teachings, God works within us to give us the desire, the will and the ability to do his work and serve his people.

This is exemplified in the therapy dog work we did. The faces of those we visited lit up with joy and surprise and pure pleasure at the site of a dog visiting with them. It's joyful to be part of something that puts smiles on the faces of others.

Is there someone you need to contact today? Can you call or send a note? A hand-written note in today's technological world can be a special blessing. Romans 15:1–2 says that "We who are strong ought to bear with the failings of the weak and not to please ourselves." Each of us should please others simply for their good, to build them up.

Who can you comfort today just as someone comforted you in your past? Consider how you can light up someone's face with your gift of love.

Gail with Sadie as we start our work as Karing Partners

Chapter 10: Getting Started

After a not-so-gentle nudge to develop a therapy dog program, I got started.

Up till now, I hadn't realized there was an interest in therapy dogs at the hospital where I worked. More importantly, I had no idea there were people right there who were willing and able to do this work with me. Therapy dog work had been around long enough that research studies were being published that supported their presence in several settings, and therapy dogs were becoming more common. But things like infection control, administrative support and acceptance by the general hospital staff were topics I felt would be a big hurdle. I knew the hospital was going to want to see valid information to back any such proposal.

The University of California at Los Angeles has a People to Animal therapy dog program and website. On their website, they present findings from numerous research studies that support the presence of animals in a hospital setting. "Reduced anxiety, comfort, lowering of blood pressure and respirations are only a few of the many benefits of the animal-human connection people experience while in a hospital".[12]

There are many places today where you can find information about starting a therapy dog program in a hospital, but they were few and far between back in 2008. So where was I going to get the support I'd need to get this off the ground? How I was going to pull off something of this scale was beyond my imagination at that moment. I talked to several people to get a feel for the atmosphere at the hospital for starting such a program. I knew a few people in hospital administration and put a bug in their ear to see what kind of resistance there might be. The feedback I got was to go ahead: Nothing ventured, nothing gained, and nothing lost as long as I was willing to do the work!

I began my research. What did therapy dogs look like in a hospital setting, what were the requirements for the dog and human member, and how do you get something like this started? I found out our sister hospital had a therapy dog program that had been in existence a few years by that time. It sounded like it was well-accepted.

After many calls and emails, I found the name of the nurse who was in charge of the program there. She was hard to catch as she was a surgical nurse and not readily available. When I finally caught her, I told her what I was thinking about.

I introduced myself and then inquired, "Paula, how did you get your therapy dog program started?"

She told me she had an incredible love for animals and, like me, had watched lots of Animal Planet shows about therapy dogs in a hospital. She went on to explain, "I worked for about two years gathering all my information. Then I heard about a program in Chicago, which was one of the first to have a hospital therapy dog program, and they invited me to come and see what they were doing." The Chicago group had provided Paula with a wealth of information, and she went home and went to work on getting a program started.

"So how did you get this finally up and running at the hospital?" I asked.

"I finally realized the oversight of these programs resided in the volunteer department," she explained. "So I spoke with the volunteer manager here. She was very excited and supported the plan, and then we worked together. I don't think I could have done it by myself.

She was essential to be getting it off the ground." As we talked further, Paula indicated, yes it had been a lot of work, but it was worth it.

"Why the volunteer department?" I asked.

"Anyone doing therapy dog work in a hospital has to do it as a volunteer," she explained. There are some exceptions today, but back in 2008, the work was done only on a volunteer basis. "We have several employees who are part of the program; they all do the therapy dog visits on their own time. At the time, the volunteer manager was supportive, and our working together brought our doggie program into place much more quickly."

The volunteer manager's role placed her in close connection with administration, so as they worked to develop their Paws for Healing therapy dog program, she was communicating the plan with the administrators along the way. They were able to get quick approval. But the big clincher was this: They found someone in the volunteer department who knew someone who knew someone, and they were able to procure a grant worth thousands and thousands of dollars to get this off the ground!

"Hah!" I laughed. "There's no way my hospital will do that. I was told to go ahead and move forward, but no dollars would be forthcoming. So what other ideas do you have?"

"Why don't you come here sometime and see the program in operation. I can show you what we've put together and what it takes to do this. Then you can decide if you want to go forward."

A few weeks later I set aside a three-day weekend and spent it watching and taking notes about everything they did. They had a well-written manual with veterinary oversight and approved by the hospital leadership medical staff. With part of the money they received from the grant, they obtained assistance to write their manual and for someone to assist them to train, test, and then graduate ten therapy dog teams over a weekend! *Whoa,* I thought, *there is no way I can do this!*

I went home exceedingly overwhelmed, but a part of me was exceedingly excited. How in heaven's name was I going to approach this monumental task? At least I had a better idea of what it was going to take. I had to decide whether I was ready to put in the time and effort to get this started. Yes, Michelle offered to help, but it was likely a one-person job to do the ground-level work of writing the manual. I figured once that was done, the rest would somehow fall into place. *Aha,* I thought, *that is where Michelle can help. I'll write the manual, and she can help brainstorm ways to get all the remaining steps in place to make this dream a reality!*

As I sat down, I thought, *Where do I start?* All I had from Paula was lots of notes. I was stumped thinking about how to get it organized. Then I thought back to the PAWS program and remembered the manual that Gretchen, our PAWS coordinator from the church, had put together many years before. I found the manual and got started. I was amazed, again, to see how organized Gretchen was! Many of the elements in her manual fit perfectly with what I needed for the manual I was writing for the hospital. I began reading and writing.

As I wrote, I thought about Karen and what I'd seen watching her and her dogs. That's when I decided. This would be a personal mission for me and a gift to Karen. It came to me. I'd name the program after Karen. Karing Partners. *Caring*, spelled with a K for Karen. And *Partners* because that's what we were. My dog and I were partners in this work, work that could not be done without the other. I'd also do this in memory of Gretchen, for without her mentorship, none of this would be possible.

I worked on the manual for over nine months. When I completed it, I dedicated it to the memory of Karen and in thanks to Gretchen. Others were immensely helpful too: Michelle, who gave me the push to start the program; Pam, one of the nurse volunteers with us at go-live but also immensely helpful in other ways; my veterinarian, Dr. Bernie Bleem. As the saying goes, "It takes a village to raise a child," so it also goes: it takes a village to start a well-planned therapy dog program!

I stayed in contact with administration about my progress. They were open to the possibility but only after all the legwork was done. Meanwhile, Max and I continued to visit three to four times a month on the transitional care unit. This helped me stay motivated about all the writing I was doing. I often thought, *Is all this work important enough to keep moving forward?* The answer was always a resounding yes!

I wrote and rewrote the manual many times. I was obsessed with making sure it addressed everything that would be needed to be approved. By this time, I'd also begun working with the volunteer manager. I took care of the doggie side of things and she took care of the people side of things. She'd heard of similar activities at other hospitals and was willing to do whatever it took to make this happen. So, armed with all of this, I marched forward.

I felt like I had a lot on the line if this didn't go well. I risked losing the visit opportunities that Max and I'd enjoyed for nearly six years visiting the transitional care unit. I was concerned that if it didn't fly now, it might be a barrier to a similar program being considered in the future. Finally, the time came for approval.

When I appeared at the meeting that day, I was in awe of what happened. This was a catholic hospital, and meetings started with a prayer. The CEO, the medical director and the director of nursing were there, among others, and many were animal lovers. They were familiar with the work I was doing and encouraged me along the way. In the prayer that morning, I remember they prayed for the group to be diligent about their consideration for the program and the effect it might have on those we visited. I was in awe as I had just prayed a similar prayer before the meeting! God answers prayers. By the end of the meeting, Karing Partners was approved. I was on cloud nine!

During the months I was working on the Karing Partners manual, the hospital was introducing a facility-wide electronic medical record (EMR). It was a huge endeavor with trainers from the vendor and other hospitals using this same EMR. Knowing a go-live for the EMR was scheduled about six months from the day Karing Partners was approved, the recommendation was to go live with Karing Partners during the go-live of the EMR. The proposition was the dogs might, and hopefully would, provide stress relief to staff and trainers alike. The thought was to start Karing Partners by first reaching out to employees, a sort of trial period. We could work out the kinks before we started visiting patients and families.

The stress of writing the manual and getting it approved was gone. Now I was charged with getting the people and dogs ready. I was excited and nervous all at the same time. My mother had always told me, "Be careful what you ask for, 'cause you just might get it." I think I saw her smile from heaven as I got my approval and started to fret about actually getting things up and running. But most of all, I knew Karen would be pleased.

Paws for Reflection

Isaiah tells us the people of Israel felt hopeless because their nation was conquered, the temple destroyed and they found themselves in exile in a foreign land. God spoke to them and said, "See, I am doing a new thing! Now it springs up; do you not perceive? I am making a way in the wilderness and streams in the wasteland" (Isaiah 43:19). This is a story about God doing a new thing and working behind the scenes of life to bring about new beginnings. As I look back, I see God was doing a "new thing" with Karing Partners. It was my passion for doing something to honor Karen that gave me the wherewithal to complete the work that God lead me to do.

They say timing is everything. The right people at the right time. God walks with us as we try those new things he places on our hearts. My experience with starting Karing Partners is illustrated in Proverbs 16:9, "In their hearts humans plan their course, but the Lord establishes their steps."

God helps us to try new things and provides the needed elements at just the right time. "But those who hope in the Lord will renew their strength. They will soar on wings like eagles; they will run and not grow weary, they will walk and not be faint" (Isaiah 40:31). Are you trying a new thing that will bring love and joy and hope to others? Assume that God is at work in your life. Move forward as if God is directing and leading you. Pay no attention to the voices of fear and doubt and others who may be skeptical. Be patient for God to do his work. "I can do all this through him who gives me strength" (Philippians 4:13).

Ruth with Sophie (center), and Gail with Sadie visit at the hospital as part of the newspaper story (Courtesy of *The Pantagraph*)[13]

Chapter 11: Go-Live

How do you describe the thrill of a dream coming true? To see it take place right in front of your eyes? I wondered what Karen would think of what I was doing with the dogs. I think Karen would have smiled and simply said, "What took you so long?" Karing Partners went live in August 2010 with five dogs and their handlers. During the first month, we made over twenty-five visits, and within the first year, we made over five hundred visits. What a way to start!

The Karing Partners volunteers came from a variety of backgrounds with a variety of reasons for participating. Most of the volunteers at go-live were employees. Others who joined later were involved in similar programs at other sites or simply "had always wanted to do this work." There was significant personal and financial investment for those participating, all at our own cost. The dogs needed annual health checks, up-to-date vaccinations and certification with one of the national therapy dog organizations. Some of us had invested a great deal of time in dog obedience training; others had experience in agility, rally or such activities familiar to those in the dog community. The human part of the team had requirements as a volunteer as well, such as health screening and vaccination requirements. The commitment was substantial, and some teams did not last long.

Mayo Clinic has an active volunteer therapy dog program. Their website lists a range of medical situations where a therapy dog is beneficial to the person receiving therapy dog services. This includes children having dental procedures, people in long-term care facilities, those receiving treatment for cancer, and people with anxiety and dementia. Mayo Clinic has more than a dozen dogs that provide a welcome distraction to routine hospital care and help reduce stress and anxiety.[14]

On day one of the electronic medical record (EMR) go-live in September 2010, Karing Partners had teams ready to get started. We'd scheduled two Karing Partners teams each day for the first week of the medical record go-live. While we'd prepared and reviewed as much as we could, we still did not know exactly what to expect. When the dog teams talked about our experiences in the weeks following the go-live, we all agreed on one thing: The dogs were a huge success!

Max and I and Michelle and her Max were scheduled for the first day. We figured it was a good idea for us to be the first off the diving board. We signed in and made sure we had hand gel to clean the hands of those who'd pet the dogs. We had note pads and pens to keep track of any notes we wanted to jot down.

"Are you ready?" I said to Michelle and Max as I did a last-minute hair check in the mirror of the sign-in room.

"Ready as we're gonna be. Let's get started!" Michelle said excitedly.

Max and Max seemed to exude their version of excitement too. Tails lifted, lots of wags, a sniff here and a sniff there, eyes bright and alert watching everything we did. I'm sure they could sense our moods and our sense of adventure. I always wondered what went through the doggies' minds as we visited. New sights and sounds and smells, lots of people to meet and our high spirits. A veritable doggie delight!

As we walked down the hallway to our assigned area, we were stopped by staff and visitors excited to meet Max and Max. Some had seen the fliers announcing our visits, others were taken by surprise. The boys were well behaved and seemed to inhale all the activity. One of the requirements of being a therapy dog is to behave appropriately when approached and pet by strangers, and Michelle and I were very proud of how the dogs performed.

"What's this? A dog in the hospital?" a visitor asked skeptically.

"Yes," Michelle explained. "It's part of a new program we just started here at the hospital. It's called Karing Partners. All the dogs have a special certificate that indicates they've been through lots of training and evaluation to do this work."

By now a few others had stopped to see what was going on. Michelle went on to explain, "We're here today as volunteers, but both Gail and I are employees of the hospital. We know lots of people; we know the layout of floors and offices and we're comfortable being here. These are our family dogs. So, because we're comfortable here, the dogs are taking a cue from us to be comfortable too."

"They're both so well behaved. And look how their scarves match your shirt," the onlookers noted cheerfully. By now both dogs were being patted on the head, and one gentleman was talking to my Max as Michelle was speaking. Max just gazed at him, lovin' every minute of the attention and acting like he knew just what the guy was saying.

The guy talking to Max pointed out, "He feels soft and they're both so fluffy."

I jumped in to explain. "An important part of our dog program is infection control. All our dogs are very clean when they come to visit. They're required to have a bath a day or two before they come, and we practice lots of hand hygiene during our visits."

I went on to tell him how my Max loves his spa get-ready day; how we'd taken a children's plastic pool, cut a hole in the center, and place it over the drain in the basement. My husband created a special area where we could put the "bath pool" with a long hose attached to the basement sink.

Our baths were a sight to behold. The setup in the basement worked great, except that it required me to be in the pool with Max. I'd gather our supplies, which included three big towels, dog shampoo, a hair dryer and a short leash I used to keep Max in the little bath pool. While he tolerated the bath, he'd prefer to skip it altogether. I'd tell him, "it's bath time," put the leash on him and he'd reluctantly follow me downstairs. Everything was set up so we could get this done as quickly as possible. Just before he stepped in the pool, I'd strip down to my underwear. After our first few sessions of bathing in the basement, I discovered he would shake constantly during the bath to get water off him. That was when I figured it was simply easier if I didn't have too many clothes on during the process since they got soaked anyway. I'd get him all soaped and rinsed and it was done. Of course, he'd shake once again as I turned off the water. We moved to a dry part of the basement where he'd patiently let me dry him off. Now we were getting to the part he really liked. When we left the basement, he'd run throughout the house and shake again! There's a lot of water on a heavily coated eighty-five-pound dog. After that, he'd lie down on the living room floor where I'd dry him with towels and the hair dryer. Oh, he did love that. With all the rubbing and the warm dryer; I think sometimes I heard him purr like a kitty cat!

I wanted the visitors to know the doggies were clean! But I only told the visitors the short version of our bathing adventure. One lady remarked, "I'm glad to hear they get special care since they're such special visitors. I, for one, am pleased to see you're bringing the dogs to see people in the hospital. I know I'd like a doggie visit if I was a patient in the hospital."

We continued the walk to our designated area and had more interactions like this from visitors and staff alike.

We started our work that day at a location designated as the Central Intelligence area for the EMR, where trouble-shooters, trainers and computer fixer-uppers were housed. It was the main area where those going out to the units to troubleshoot would be meeting, and part of our strategic plan was that the group would spread the word about the dogs being there to visit that day.

When the Maxes and Michelle and I entered the training room, Michelle and her Max went one way and we went the other. People stopped what they were doing to pet and interact with the dogs. We tried to be strict about using the hand gel for each person before they touched the dogs, but often they were so quick to reach out and touch the dogs it was hard to get the hygiene step in. Over time we got better about using the hand gel before people touched the dogs, but we were pleased with the positive reaction we'd received.

Armed with confidence from our initial interaction, we went out to our designated units and walked the hallways where nurses and doctors and therapists were getting final training tips for the EMR and working out installation issues. Almost every time we approached someone, we were well received. The biggest accomplishment for the day was the positive reception we had from some of the most influential physicians. For me, as a nurse working with many of these physicians for so many years, it was fun to see them stop their work and pet Max and interact with me and the dogs on a very personal level. They'd talk about their dogs and how their dogs would or would not be able to do this work. We were thanked again and again. It was fun to see people be so surprised and so into what we were doing. However, not everything was hunky-dory.

"What are you doing?" a nurse snarled. "Why are these dogs in the hospital? A hospital is no place for a dog to visit!" Well, I certainly got her message loud and clear.

I explained our purpose, our training and the hygiene efforts we had in place. We were hopeful that the strict cleaning and bathing protocols would win her over, as well as others who weren't so keen about the dog's presence. We had a few other naysayers that day, but overall, most were quite excited about our new endeavor. This particular nurse, and a few others, took a long time to change their mind about a hospital not being a place for a dog to visit. I believe what finally won them over was the positive response we received from others, especially the patients and visitors. Many times, while doing our regular paid job, Michelle and I and others would be asked when and where the dogs were coming next, and they made it a point to come and see us when we visited.

Others in the Karing Partners group talked about similar experiences during our initial week's visits. The best news is it simply went well. And it was what we needed to get our final full medical staff and administrative approval.

Over time, staff, patients and families who received visits, including physicians and some of the administrators, told us how much they loved the dog visits. "I'm doing better now that Max came to see me," "Such a great service," "I miss my dog" were among some of the comments we heard. Volunteers and employees said: "Your visits made my day!" Many wished the dogs would come every day. A nurse once told me, after Max and I visited with a hospice patient and his family that our visit brought a lift to the spirits of everyone there that day. A Karing Partner volunteer said, "We were stopped several times by people wanting to pet the dog before I even got to sign in!" One physician stated, "I want to tell you how I appreciate the Karing Partners program. It brightens my day to see the dogs. I think for most patients the hospital is a foreign, strange place. The dogs give a release from the anxiety of being in the hospital and bring something they can relate to and makes them feel comfortable. I hope we continue the program."

Karing Partners volunteered in a variety of events. Of course, visiting patients and families was the priority. But the employees enjoyed the visits just as much. Based on this, Karing Partners were offered the chance to be present as a de-stress break at Employee Wellness events. We'd be placed in a special area of the Wellness Event where employees could come and pet the dogs. Participation in various hospital week events and other activities with employees was well received, and requests for more were common.

The annual employee education event provided another adventure for the dogs. Each year nurses, therapists, aides and others involved with direct patient care were required to complete an annual skills validation. It was a simulated situation where they'd be asked to review and demonstrate proficiency with high-risk patient care interventions, infection control, specialty equipment and such. The dogs provided a quick mental break from their activities and allowed the staff members to relax and chill for just a moment before returning to their daily tasks.

But even after all this, I was still wondering, *Do our visits make a difference to the patients?* After all, our primary plan was for the program to impact patients and their families. Shortly after starting Karing Partners, I received my validation. Max and I were visiting the step-down intensive care unit, where patients are transferred when they are no longer critically ill.

Mary Jo, a nurse on the unit, stopped me, "Hi, Max. It's so good to see you. It's been sorta crazy here the last few days; I can sure use some doggie love." You notice she didn't say hi to *me*! It was a common response most of us received. Mary Jo and I talked for a while as she pet Max.

As Mary Jo and I were talking and Max was greeting the staff, the daughter of one of the patients came out of the room to visit with us. She was quite emotional. She walked up to Max, and after asking permission, bent over and hugged him. Her mom was a patient on the unit who'd recently had a major stroke. We talked for a while about what she was experiencing with her aging mother. The daughter told me she wished they could see some sign of life left in her mom. She wanted to know, even just one last time, if her mom was still there, if she was hearing and knowing about the family's presence.

"Can you possibly bring Max into the room and just see if Mom has any awareness at all? She loves dogs. We had lots of dogs in our home when I was growing up. I'd love if something like this might wake her up," she pleaded. The nurses nodded their approval.

"Of course, we can come in and visit," I offered. "But please don't put too much emphasis on what might or might not happen." I was willing to visit with Max, but I was skeptical about any response to Max based on what the daughter and the nursing staff had indicated.

"Hi, this is Max," I said as we walked into the room. The granddaughter was sitting in the back of the room. "Max is here to say hi to everyone. Would you like to pet him?" I asked as Max walked to the back of the room where the granddaughter was sitting on the love seat.

"Oh, Max, I'm so glad you came to see us. We needed a special visitor like you right now," she said softly as she reached out to grasp Max's coat.

The daughter went over and also sat on the love seat. They talked animatedly about the dogs in their life and, like most other rooms we visited, they showed me pictures of their dogs. They talked about the dogs Grandma had over the years; how the entire family was dog lovers because of Grandma. We talked in normal voice tones and laughed often. I suspected that if Grandma was able to hear, she likely heard the banter and the laughs.

It was time for Max to meet Grandma. I positioned Max next to her bed. The daughter sat on her mom's bed and started talking to her mom about their family dogs, reminiscing about their antics and how they miss their dogs. Max was a big goldie—he weighed over eighty-five pounds—so when he stood next to the patient's bed, his large head was at the height of the mattress.

The daughter introduced Max to Grandma. He laid his chin on the bed. The daughter carefully moved her mom's hand to stroke Max's head as she talked. We stood like this for five or six minutes with the daughter constantly talking and helping Grandma stroke Max's head. Suddenly the patient started moving her fingers on Max's head as the daughter helped her stroke Max. The daughter looked at me with her eyes wide open in shock and whispered, "She's moving her fingers!"

The granddaughter came running over to the side of the bed to see this and then went out to the nurses' station to get one of the nurses. We all stood in amazement as Max did his miracles. It wasn't much, but it was something! The daughter and granddaughter were thrilled beyond words.

Max and I left the room shortly after. We stayed on the unit for a few more visits. Just as we were leaving, the daughter came up to us in tears. She thanked us over and over for being there and for being a part of what we just observed. "You'll never know what this has meant to me. Just to see that she was still there and responded helps me to know that all my being here and talking to her matters."

Maybe we were making a difference. Another illustration of this was a bring-a-smile visit we had with a patient who had numerous visitors in the room. One of the visitors was a young child about six months old. The family had big dogs at home so the little one was not one bit afraid of Max. When he saw Max, he let out a giggle and made cooing noises that could be heard down the hall. I remember two nurses coming down to see what the party was about. They simply smiled, enjoyed a moment of pure joy and then went back to their work. We stayed for about an hour. We usually tried to limit our visits to about ten or twenty minutes so that we could make our rounds to other patients. But that day there was so much joy in the moment; even Max was not ready to leave!

It was evident our visits were making a positive difference to many of those we served. We loved hearing the good feedback from patients, visitors and employees alike. Those of us on the human side of this partnership enjoyed it immensely, and we all felt our doggies did too. We watched as our dogs pranced around with their ears up and tails a-waggin', bright eyes and doggie smiles when beckoned by employees and visitors. Over the next few years, our program expanded, and we gained many new human and furry friends along the way. It was evident we were all enjoying what we were doing: patients, families, dogs and handlers. Doesn't get much better than that!

Paws for Reflection

A lifetime of my faith, putting trust in the Lord, my love of helping people and my love of dogs has shown me how beautifully things can work together in ways I never thought possible. The joy of seeing the love of God reflected in the work of our dogs has been amazing! I experienced joy watching mine and others' dogs as they did this awesome work. The joy we have given so many people over the years is well beyond anything I could have imagined.

I am still not sure exactly where one story stops and a new one begins. It simply all flows together. The Bible says in Psalm 37:5 to "commit your way to the Lord, trust in him and he will do this." All I can say is that the Lord did it: the people I met, who they introduced me to, how the next step simply fell into place. Once we started, it seemed to flow, as in Matthew where he says, "No one lights a lamp and then puts it under a basket. Instead, a lap is placed on a stand, where it gives light to everyone in the house" (5:15 NLT).

Is there something sitting on your heart that you've been thinking about getting started or involved in? Have you prayed and asked God to direct your ways? Don't be afraid to take a few steps and ask for help. Many impossible ideas are made possible in Christ. The Bible tells us in Ezekiel 36:26, "I will give you a new heart and put a new spirit in you."

Gail with Sadie (front) and Laura with Moose, as we sign in at the volunteer area

Chapter 12: Sadie

When Karing Partners was only a year old, I lost my Max to cancer. I was shocked. He was getting older, but we still walked almost two miles every day! I recall the day we walked, and all of a sudden, he stopped and sat down. He couldn't walk. At eighty-five pounds, I couldn't carry him, so I ever so slowly encouraged and helped him walk the half-mile home. I called Dr. Bleem and we took him right in. An X-ray showed a lesion on his back leg. Dr. Bleem took a biopsy, and then called a few hours later with the grim news. It was bone cancer. We opted for no surgery, just comfort measures. For a few short weeks, Max was enrolled in a research study at the University Veterinarian School. We went weekly for shots and embraced the time we had left. One day, as we arrived at the university, his exuberance at seeing those who were so nice to him caused him to jump and put extra weight on his leg, and the bone snapped. We put him down that day. My first official therapy dog was now in doggie heaven. My heart was broken.

Max had shown me the thrilling world of therapy dog work. And the presence I felt with Karen as I did my visits and talked about why I did this work made me realize I was not done with therapy dog work. So I pondered only briefly before I decided I wanted another therapy dog.

While I was mourning the loss of Max, I remained active in Karing Partners doing office work in the volunteer department. About this time, the hospital brought in a new manager of volunteers. She was excited about the program and interested in seeing the program grow. She and many others were instrumental in my getting another therapy dog.

Marcia, a friend from church, was an active member of both PAWS and Karing Partners. She and her dog Amber, another golden retriever, visited regularly for both activities. I got a call from her shortly after Max died.

"Hi," Marcia said softly. "I'm so sorry to hear about Max. Look at all of the wonderful things you and Max accomplished."

"Thanks, Marcia," I replied. "I miss him so much and I miss being involved in the doggie work."

"You and Max were so active with PAWS and Karing Partners," she noted, "I hope you don't plan to stop. Have you thought about getting another dog?"

I hesitated a bit and then replied, "Yes. We are going to get another dog. Mostly because I just love my therapy dog work and don't feel like I'm done with that in my life yet. But I'm going to rest my heart a while first."

Marcia paused, but not for long. She was on a mission. "I know it's only been a few weeks. But I know a family who has a lovely, lively eighteen-month-old golden retriever. She is a handful. They'd been in a house with a fence with lots of room to run, but now they're in a condo with no fence. The dog is a bit more than they can handle right now, and she's a runner." Marcia went on to tell me the family had tried to find a rescue for the dog, but all the rescues were full and this family wanted to find the dog a home as soon as possible.

It was Monday. My husband was out of town that week with friends on a golf outing. So now what do I do? I told Marcia I'd go and see the dog, but not until tomorrow. I called my husband and told him the circumstances with the dog. Both of us knew we wanted another dog, but were we ready yet? Did we need more time to grieve and adjust? We decided I'd go and visit. But my husband made it quite clear: just visit and no commitments.

Tuesday came and I went to visit. Marcia had set up a time for our meeting so the family knew I was coming. I parked in the driveway and turned off the car when a lovely but lively golden retriever bounded out the front door. A relatively large man came running out of the house attached to this dog that was pulling him along about a hundred miles an hour! As I got out of the car, the dog came running at me full speed and proceeded, I guess, to say hello. She wiggled and wagged, tried to a get a whiff of every part of me and jumped all over me. *Oh my,* I thought, *am I ready for this level of activity?* I don't think I'd ever seen Max this excited and out of control in all the years we had him. *And,* I told myself, *don't forget that you and David are no spring chickens!* Could we handle this dog?

"This is Sadie," he said a bit out of breath. "She has quite a bit of energy." Really? Like I needed this pointed out to me.

"I can see she is certainly energetic. Tell me about her," I inquired, trying to get hold of Sadie to pet her and make some good contact with her.

Marcia had told me a little about the family and why they needed to find a home for Sadie. The man filled me in on a few more things. They'd lived in a home with a fence when they got her as a puppy and even then she was a handful. "She'd climb the fence and we had to go around the neighborhood and look for her," he said. "When we moved here we couldn't find a home with a fence. So now we tie her up outside. She's gotten out of the house several times and once was gone for two days before neighbors helped us get her back."

We talked more and a neighbor came over with his dog. Sadie and the dog played and seemed to get along. He told me they took Sadie to their daughter's baseball games and she did well with people and dogs in that setting.

"We're so busy and no one is home most of the time. We just don't feel right keeping her locked up all day. The way she runs, I feel like she needs a place where she can run off her high level of energy."

My heart was won over. I was ready to consider, but David had asked me to wait until he got home to commit to taking her. I explained this to the family.

"I'd like to think about this and talk to my husband. I need a bit of time to think more since we just lost Max six weeks ago. What if I talk to my husband and, if we decide to take her, I'll pick her up on Saturday and bring her home?"

The man paused. He said he had another home for Sadie, a home in the country where she'd have acres and acres to run. It was clear if I did not take Sadie today, she'd be gone.

I'm not one to usually make a hasty decision, but I did that day. I decided to take Sadie home with me. *Oh dear, what am I doing? Is this the right decision?* I sent up a few prayers asking for forgiveness that I was going against my husband's wishes. I hastily thought if he doesn't agree to keep her, we'd go about finding another home for her. I knew enough people in town to help us out with a home for her if it did not work out. But what was I going to tell David?

So Sadie and I got in the car and came home. All the while she was bounding and jumping around in the backseat. The more she bounded and jumped the more I thought, *Oh my, what have I done?* Sadie and I attempted to get settled at home. They'd given us all her things, including her kennel. I was grateful they'd given us all these items because in my grief I had given away all of Max's things. I'd sort of planned that if we got another dog, it would be a smaller dog, something I would be better able to handle. Sadie weighed only sixty-two pounds compared to Max's eighty-five pounds, but I wondered if I could handle those sixty-two pounds of high energy. As I watched her the rest of the afternoon, I pondered: *What am I going to do when David calls?* I planned my conversation. I was *not* going to lie about having her home, since he had explicitly asked me to wait. But I thought, *I just won't tell him everything.*

He called me that evening. Our conversation went something like this: "I met Sadie today. She's eighteen months old and very active. Yes, she appears to be healthy. The family loves her but she is just more than they can handle. Of course I'll think about it." Now you note I never said she was home with me. But you see, he never asked.

In the meantime, Sadie and I went about the rest of our day and first night. I was pleasantly surprised by how well she went into her kennel at bedtime. In the morning we took a walk along the same paths I'd walked both Tucker and Max. And she met all the neighbors. I told them how Sadie would not be with me if I'd waited till Saturday, and I confessed the phone call with my husband, how he did not know she was with me. That "we were going to decide on Saturday whether we would keep her or not." They all knew David was out of town. So they banded together and said a prayer for us to make things go right. Whatever "right" was, they were going to ask for "right." But in all truth, the neighborhood had decided that Sadie should stay!

I talked to David that evening.

"How's the golfing going?" I asked in an animated voice. I thought, *If I'm perky, he won't ask questions I don't want to answer.*

"Going good. Great weather today but the course was crowded," he went on, telling me everything except how his golfing was. Most golfers don't like to talk about the state of their game unless it exceeds expectations.

"Good to hear. When are you coming home?" I hoped he wasn't thinking of coming home early.

"On Saturday, as we planned. So what are your thoughts about the dog?" There he goes—right to the point.

Okay, I thought. *No more stalling.* "Well, I need to tell you the whole story. Sadie's here with me. She's been here since Tuesday afternoon. You never asked if she was here! You just asked questions about her and I answered them." I was feeling a bit contrite by now.

"But the reason I could answer them, was 'cause she was here with me." I could hear him tell the guys in the background that Sadie was at the house. I heard the laughs and the shouts in the background.

I went on. "I know you told me not to take her until this weekend. But if I hadn't taken her then, they were going to move her to a farm way out in the country where she was just going to run," I was rambling by now. "She is a bit energetic, but she seems to have a sweet disposition. And she already does sit and lay down for me." I continued to babble on about stories I'd been told about Sadie.

"I know you asked me not to take her till you could meet her. I called a few places and people the last couple of days, and we do have some options to find her another home," I told him and added, "if we need to." I could hear the guys laughing and telling David it was a lost cause. Sadie was ours.

He actually got a hoot out of my story. Especially when I told him that the neighbors had all decided that we should keep Sadie. He took it all in stride and said he was not surprised that I'd taken Sadie that very first night knowing she'd be a runner in the country. The guys he was with teased him mercilessly that the neighbors had contrived to be on my side. We still chuckle today about this story and his willingness to be outvoted by the neighbors.

It quickly became evident Sadie needed direction and lots of training. When we went for walks in those first months, there were a few times she pulled me off my feet in her attempt to chase a squirrel, a deer, a bird or whatever was moving. What a change from Mellow Max!

We started our dog obedience classes in September. I'd taught two of the PAWS classes by this time, but there was nothing I'd gleaned in those two classes I was able to use with Sadie. While we waited to start our dog class, I checked out all I could about training high-energy dogs. We worked on the basics of sit and stay. I discovered as long as I had a treat Sadie would sit well. It was the stay she simply thought was unnecessary. I was grateful when training classes started.

I was better at classes this time around. Since I'd discovered Sadie loved to work for her treats, we used lots of treats for training and I just cut back on the amount of food we fed for her morning and evening meals. We moved quickly through the training and took each class just once this time around. Apparently, I did learn something from my classes with Max!

Sadie was very responsive to training. But she was also very fast. When she sat, she sat *fast*. When she went down, she went down *fast*. When she heeled, she heeled *fast*. You get the picture. She did everything *fast*. It was a bit overwhelming for me, but the instructors loved her quick response and would often ask to use her as an example in our class on how to engage the dog to get the response they were looking for.

Because Sadie was a quick study with her classes, and since I had the background with my therapy dog work with Max, after completing our advanced obedience class, we went straight into Canine Good Citizen class. I decided to use this for preliminary training for her therapy dog test.

We passed both the CGC and our therapy dog test the first time around. I noticed when Sadie was being coached and we were engaged together in something, she was very responsive and listened well. Even though she was still highly active, she seemed to be able to channel her energy when needed, so I decided we were ready to join Karing Partners and PAWS.

Sadie evolved into a Karing Partner quite readily. I was amazed at how well she did as a three-year-old in her Karing Partners work. As I'd done with Max, we had a special routine of getting dressed and ready to go *to work*. She seemed to understand what we were doing and the need for her to quiet down. She settled nicely and listened well as we made our visits. For the kids at The Baby Fold, we were back to a bit more active dog, which of course the kids loved. At the hospital, she was able to contain her energy and turn on her chill moves. However, even to this day she has trouble controlling her desire to see someone up close and personal when they call her name or talk to her.

"What a lovely dog you have there. What's her name?" people asked me as we walked by.

"Be careful. Her name is Sadie. But if you say her name or talk to her, you *will* be required to pet her," I warned them with a smile.

"Okay, Sadie, come here and let me feel how soft you are," or some such words usually followed. Sadie loved the attention and people loved her responsiveness. I always kept myself alert to this part of her behavior, especially at the hospital. A hospital is not a good place for a big dog to move quickly. She was also a leaner. She loved being touched and she leaned on people as they loved on her. I think she figured this made people love on her longer. I enjoyed hearing people exclaim, "Look, she's leaning on me. She must know how much I love dogs."

So Sadie took over the role in Karing Partners that Max had left empty. I'd thought no dog would ever be as wonderful a therapy dog as Mellow Max. But over the years, Sadie's love for people and her exuberance have made her an amazing therapy dog. Sadie's endurance level allowed us to sometimes spend as much as two or more hours at the hospital. It allowed us to try things Max simply didn't have the energy or interest to do.

One of the employee events Sadie and I thought was special was the annual staff education. Having been a nurse for a very long time and remembering the years when I worked the night shift from 11:00 p.m. to 7:00 a.m., I had a special heart for those working the overnight hours. Each year the education department held one education event on the night shift, education from 2:00 a.m. to 4:00 a.m. I scheduled my work hours around this event so Sadie and I could participate.

The alarm would go off at 12:30 a.m. Sadie was a bit perplexed about why we were getting up and going somewhere at that hour, but she was willing. By 1:00 a.m., we were on the road. When we arrived at 1:30 a.m., our first job was to walk around the hospital and remind the employees of the education event, which included food and a dog. By 2:00 a.m., employees would mosey on down. Sadie and I were the greeters. For the next two hours, we'd greet, walk around, meet staff and provide lots of lovin'. Sadie never lost a beat, never got tired and never needed a rest. By 4:00 a.m., the employees were back on the units and we'd close up shop. When we arrived home at about 4:30 a.m., we both went right to bed.

"So tell me . . ." Brittany queried me one night after completing her night shift education review. She was an RN in ICU. She'd heard about the dogs, but her encounter with Sadie was her first. ". . . Just how does one become a therapy dog?"

"Well, it starts with a couple of things," I explained. "First your dog needs to like people, be willing and interested in working with you and following your directions. Then it takes the time to either self-train or take classes so your dog can do the basic sit, stay and come. When that's in good shape, you take the therapy dog test."

"I have two black labs. One sounds like she'd be perfect for this. My older lab, Mary Kay, and I would love to do this; it's been a dream of mine. How would I get started?" she asked.

I knew she was a busy lady. She had a young child and worked full-time in the ICU on the night shift. But if she was interested, I'd help her. I reviewed the steps she'd need to take. I also gave her the Alliance of Therapy Dogs website. It's the association where I was a therapy dog evaluator. I encouraged her to check out the site and see what she and Mary Kay needed to do to pass their test. I'd become a therapy dog evaluator by that time and told her I could test her and Mary Kay whenever they were ready. I also offered for her to observe me and Sadie when we visited one day to see exactly what we did and what Mary Kay would be doing as a therapy dog, just to see if this was what she wanted.

Brittany went home and did her homework. She observed one day when Sadie and I did some visits. I was able to demonstrate for her the various testing behaviors as well as Sadie's interaction with patients and visitors, all of which Mary Kay would need to do for her test. About six months after our initial nighttime rendezvous, Brittany contacted me and said she and Mary Kay were ready. We met, completed the test and shared visit evaluations, and they passed. Brittany and Mary Kay were now the newest Karing Partners members.

I was grateful for what we'd done with PAWS and Karing Partners. And even more grateful for the positive responses we received. Author and poet Maya

Angelou shared a thought I consider as I think about our work: "I've learned that people will forget what you said, people will forget what you did, but people will never forget how you made them feel."[15] Fellow team members voiced, again and again, the joy they experienced doing this work with their dogs. We'd started Karing Partners back in 2010, and here we were nearing 2019. During those years there were over twenty-two therapy dog teams in Karing Partners. What we'd done was a result of hard work and lots of time and effort. Thinking back, I recall feeling a bit giddy; like that five-year-old who rides their two-wheeler for the first time. Yes, we worked hard but we did it!

Paws for Reflection

I don't think the Psalmist was thinking about dogs when he wrote, "Our mouths were filled with laughter, our tongues with songs of joy . . ." (126:2), but I think it applies! God placed Sadie in our lives for a good reason. But we were unsure at the time. She was a bit wild and unruly and pulled me over numerous times when we first brought her home. I remember thinking God must have quite a sense of humor in watching me with this rambunctious dog that he placed in our lives in our near-sixties! But she has brought tremendous joy, happiness and love to us and others. Sadie kept us on our toes in her early years, but today she is gentle, well behaved and loves people and dogs of all kinds.

Many Bible verses tell us that God wants us to find joy in our life. Joy rooted in who he is. The Bible teaches us that God and his word are our true source of joy. Psalm 16:11 "You make known to me the path of life; you will fill me with joy in your presence, with eternal pleasures at your right hand." As we come to know God and establish a close, personal relationship with him, we find joy and a "peace of God, which transcends all understanding" (Philippians 4:7).

What has God placed in your life that seems absurd, silly or funny? Do you find delight in what is around you? Watch your dogs or other animals, and watch their silly behaviors like Sadie's happy dance when she rolls and rolls on the grass and makes me smile. Watch animal antics on social media. Find something today that tickles your tummy and makes you smile. It pleases God when you are happy!

Sadie and Moose visit in the hallway at the hospital

Max with a buddy

Pastor Hoffman and Kate finish their
PAWS class

Sadie visits with Dick in his home

Sadie learning hand signal to wait

PART THREE

Looking Back

What you see and what you hear depends a great deal on where you are standing. It also depends on what sort of person you are.

—*C.S. Lewis*

Aidan, Karen's grandson, and Sadie know that dogs make a difference

Chapter 13: Dogs Make a Difference

Dogs have been part of my life for most of my life. Dogs mean different things to different people. Likely if you're reading this book, you're somewhat of a dog lover. So hopefully you'll agree on at least some of the reasons why I think we have dogs in our lives. They're silly and make us smile, they're loyal and make us feel important, they give us focus and a reason to get up in the morning, but most of all, they love us with a special kind of unconditional love. Therapy dog work lets us share all these attributes with others.

There were many dog breeds in PAWS and Karing Partners. PAWS saw the greatest variety. Karing Partners did not see as wide a variety, partly because of the fewer number of dogs, but maybe because of the different purpose, requirements and requested commitment of the program. Hospital therapy dog work typically seems to draw labradors and golden retrievers mainly because of their gentle dispositions. In our program, goldens outnumbered them all; in one year alone, five of the teams had golden retrievers. Other breeds included Great Pyrenees, Maltese, Havanese, labrador retrievers, poodles, Border collies, Shelties and mixed breeds of all kinds. Many of our dogs were rescues, despite their purebred breeding. Those of us who'd rescued our dogs liked to brag about how we'd taken dogs that were in great need of a home and not only gave them a home but wonderful work to do!

When doing my routine hospital rounds, I enjoyed hearing comments from staff about a recent dog visit on their unit. "Oh, I loved when Sissy came yesterday sitting in the little basket that Mary rides around in." One of my favorites was, "Cooper was here today wearing a tie! Jim got tired of everyone asking if Cooper was a boy or a girl, so he put a tie on him! He's so big and just so gentle. Patients love him."

There were times when I felt our visits were heaven-directed. A nurse told me once the timing of the Karing Partner visit was amazing. She said, "My patient got very sick and died unexpectedly. It was hard on the family and it was very hard on me. The doggie came about an hour later and when I saw the dog, I got down and hugged her and cried into her fur. I needed special doggie loving right then and there."

Some of my favorite comments were from the nurses on the orthopedic unit: "Can't you please resign from your job and just bring Sadie here full-time? We want her as our resident dog!" And "Is a dog coming today or tomorrow? The patient in room 222 could use a visit. She loves when the dogs come. I know they have to go to other floors too, but she could use a special visit."

Such wonderful affirmation for the work we were doing!

At the end of a Karing Partners visit, each team jotted down a few notes about their visits that day. The purpose was to have a record of patient rooms we'd been in but also to record the reaction of patients, visitors and employees. The room number was logged in the event of any problems or complaints, for quality and risk purposes. The notes were a great way to capture the wonderful, kind, grateful and loving responses we experienced. I sometimes worked with other teams and we'd laugh and go on about an awesome visit we experienced.

"Hi, Ruth. How'd your day go?" I asked, as Ruth and Sophie and Sadie and I met up in the volunteer room and signed out for the day.

"We had a couple of great visits today. One patient had been here a few weeks ago when we visited. He acted like Sophie was family; he was so excited to see her and remembered her name. The patient talked about his dog and how much he missed her. Before we left, they asked us to pray with them. That kind of visit makes me feel like we've done something special."

I agreed. "I taught Sadie to 'say a prayer,' and I ask her to do that on some of the visits where it just feels right. People seem to like that."

Ruth went on, "Just before coming to sign out, we stopped by the emergency department. The staff asked us to go into one of the rooms and help quiet a little girl so they could provide her treatments. The parents were so grateful we were there. They asked us to put Sophie on the bed, and Sophie helped distract the little girl while they were putting an IV into her other arm. It was a special visit."

"Awww . . . that's so nice," I said, and added, "it's pretty special when the doctors and nurses know our dogs can make a difference in reducing stress in a situation like that."

"When the doctors and nurses ask us to be involved, for me, it validates that what we do is good," Ruth noted.

We chatted a bit more, jotted down our notes and signed out. It was time to head out. The dogs were usually tired after an hour or so of visit time. I suspect being fully engaged, interacting with many different people, and being on such high alert continuously for the duration of their visit was taxing.

"Isn't it great to be able to share our dogs with so many different people?" Michelle asked me one day. "I never imagined people would enjoy the visits as much as they do. And it's the employee responses I'm astounded by. I went into this expecting patients and families might enjoy the dogs, but I never anticipated employees would enjoy it as much as they seem to. It seems to give a lift to their day."

I agreed and shared one of my recent experiences. "I was on my way to the med-surg unit when I was stopped by one of the pharmacists. They asked me to bring Sadie into their office area. In all my years of nursing, I've never been inside the hospital pharmacy; I've only stood outside to pick up meds for a patient. We go inside and just about everyone goes gah-gah over Sadie! Sadie's in seventh heaven with all those folks loving on her! She'd go to one person, and then someone else would talk sweet to her and she'd run over to that person and so on. They laughed as they saw she was enjoying the interaction as much as they were enjoying her."

"Right!" Michelle chuckled as she envisioned the scenario. "I had exactly the same experience a few weeks ago! I'm going to stop by the pharmacy every time Max and I visit. They seem so appreciative of our stopping by. And just like everywhere else we go, out came the phones to take pictures and show pictures of their dogs."

The information we provided after our visits were tallied and shared as part of the annual report. The number of visits, number of active teams and responses from those we visited, including employees, patients and visitors, were part of the report. For example, from September 2014 to September 2015, we had eleven dog teams and visited five of the hospital units as well as family waiting rooms. That year there were twenty Karing Partner's visits scheduled each month—some were solo visits, other times we visited in pairs. We put in over three-hundred and fifty hours of on-site visit time with the faithful volunteers in our group and performed more than three thousand four hundred patient and visitor contacts that year.

I was an instructor for nursing students at the hospital where I worked and did my therapy dog work. The class I taught for senior students included a type of research project, called a Change Project. I enjoyed teaching that class to see what the students would discover. The idea was to teach and encourage students to find something in their work environment they could validate, or possibly change or improve upon.

So in 2015, I decided to do my own research to discover what I could about our Karing Partner visits on a more data-driven level. I was pleased with the subjective responses we received about the program but wondered if the responses were simply sentimental based on people's love of dogs. I wondered, *Does our work possibly make a clinical difference?*

Over the years I'd read research articles on therapy dogs in hospitals. I was determined to prove to myself and others that our efforts were making a positive physiological difference in people's health, in addition to making them happy. I went through the formal research process at the medical center. It took nearly two years to develop my hypothesis and get the required thirty participants in the research group and thirty participants in the control group for my research.

My research partners were Michelle and Max. I collected data on a total of sixty patients on the orthopedic surgical unit at the hospital for over a year and a half. I asked: Does having a visit with a dog from Karing Partners improve your heart rate, respiratory rate and pain, and are you less anxious and depressed? Our research showed that people who had a dog visit experienced a reduction in their anxiety and depression score, and had a reduction in their pain score, heart rate and respiratory rate.[16]

What did I discover? Do therapy dogs make a difference for people in the hospital? My research said yes, dog visits made a difference for some people by lowering their heart rate, pain and respirations. Do they make hospitalized people feel better? My research said yes, dog visits made a clinical difference for some people by reducing their anxiety and depression. I was excited to affirm that our dogs made a positive impact on those we visited!

We were grateful when our good stories reached hospital administrators and other leaders at the hospital. One story taken to a hospital leadership meeting, with representatives from all departments, was about a little girl with severe autism. She was awaiting permanent placement in a residential facility. The staff noted that no one came to visit her. A special request went out to the therapy dog teams to try and see if a dog visit might be beneficial for her. When the dog entered, the little girl started to giggle and smile and pet the dog; it was more response than the medical team had seen from her at any time. The leadership team was so moved by this that they requested additional visits from the therapy dogs to visit this girl until her discharge. Did the dogs make a difference for this little girl? I'll let you decide.

As I look back and think about our work, my own stories and those of others, the results of my research, and what people told us, I go back to my question: Do dogs make a difference? My answer is yes. A patient once told me what the dogs meant to her when they visited her in the hospital. "The dogs make me happy. For a few moments, I'm not a patient in the hospital dealing with my health and bad news. For just a few moments I forget about the pain, the decisions I have to make and the changes I will live with when I go home. I think happy thoughts. I feel like I'm someone who's loved and not someone who needs medication or a walk down the hall. It gives me hope that I have something to look forward to when I leave here." And I think I hear Karen, somewhere in the distance, whispering, "I know just how she feels."

Paws for Reflection

Those who are dog lovers, or animal lovers of any kind, know our animals play an integral role in our lives. They love us, they support us, and they find joy in being with us. And likewise, we love and find joy in their presence. Our animals want to be part of our lives, just as God wants to be part of our lives. Do you know God also loves you, all the time? And he wants us to love others as he loves us. "Above all, clothe yourselves with love, which binds us all together in perfect harmony" (Colossians 3:14 NLT).

We're grateful if someone helps us when we're struggling. We appreciate it when others are willing to help carry our burden of pain, loneliness or loss. As believers, we help because we've heard God ask us to "carry each other's burdens, and in this way you will fulfill the law of Christ" (Galatians 6:2). When we share with those in need, we are doing the work of the Lord. The Bible tells us in Hebrews 6:10 that when we do this work, "he will not forget your work and the love you have shown him as you have helped his people."

Has God given you a heart of compassion? How might you be a blessing to others? Pray and ask for guidance to see what you can do to serve others.

Gail with Max, and Judy with Kaia demonstrate the "strange dog" greeting for CGC and therapy dog testing

Chapter 14: Therapy Dog Evaluator

When Karing Partners started, we suspected it would be a challenge to find enough teams to meet our needs as the program grew. We worked with some of the local dog training facilities, which advertised our needs, and teams slowly trickled in. Back when I was working on program development for Karing Partners and meeting people in what I call the doggie world, I toyed with the idea of becoming a therapy dog evaluator. But was I up to this new challenge? James Alfred Wright, "James Herriot," famous veterinarian, storyteller, author and animal lover extraordinaire, is known to have said, "There have been times in my life when confronted by black and hopeless circumstances,

I've discovered in myself undreamed-of resources of courage and resolution."[17] I decided to find my courage and resolution and become a therapy dog evaluator.

Pam was a good friend at work quite involved in the doggie world. She was active in obedience and agility work and a member of the local dog training facility. She and her two dogs were active in Karing Partners. I decided to broach the topic with her.

"Pam, I'm considering becoming a therapy dog evaluator. But I need way more experience with dog work than what I have. You know lots of people in the doggie world. Other than being a participant in classes for dog obedience, and the little bit I've done with PAWS, I've not done much else in the line of dog training," I said as we talked at work one day.

My investigation into becoming a therapy dog evaluator made me realize I was lacking in most of the requirements. I told her, "The application says I need to have knowledge of a variety of dog work over many years, such as obedience training, even dog show judging, and know about all sorts of dog breeds." As I looked back at my experience, I scored a zero in most categories. Pretty much the only breeds that I was familiar with were my three golden retrievers and the poodles I had as a child.

"I might be able to help you out with some of that. Let me think and make some phone calls," she promised.

About a week later, we got together and she had a plan. Pam is one of those people who always has a plan. Especially when it came to anything with dogs.

"I found some people who are willing to let you help as a backup assistant with agility competition. We always need someone willing to help set up the agility route and keep the group going so we don't lose time when it's their turn to compete." I was thankful she was able to come up with something so quickly.

For the next six months, I went to various dog agility competitions. I helped with the trail setups and did traffic control for teams waiting for their turn. I'd drive as far as fifty miles or more if a competition was on a weekend that worked with my schedule.

Pam also introduced me to people at the local dog training center, many of whom I'd known as instructors. This community introduced me to a few additional activities that helped give me the background I needed for my evaluator application.

Finally, the time came to submit my application. It reminded me of my school days when I wrote lengthy papers and I was up against pass or fail! I had to answer the questions and then show examples of how I met the required criteria. I submitted a seven-page essay answering questions as to how I'd worked with a variety of dog breeds, what I would do if the dog became aggressive with another dog during a test, and how I might counsel a team that did not meet the requirements of the test. I also needed recommendations from three people who knew me and my work with dogs. I believe the most instrumental evidence of acceptability was the work I'd done creating Karing Partners. My work with PAWS and exposure to agility and other training further supported my application. About two weeks after I submitted the application, I received a call from the Alliance of Therapy Dogs for a fifteen-minute interview. During the interview, I was told they'd accepted me as an evaluator and I could start testing immediately. I was thrilled! Another new adventure in my work with therapy dogs!

I reached out to an established therapy dog evaluator in the area, and she graciously allowed me to observe her conducting therapy dog evaluations. She was exceedingly helpful; she coached me and gave some great tips. I'm indebted to her mentoring and welcoming me to this new world I found myself in.

For my first solo evaluation, I was in a quandary as to where to conduct the test and the visits. I'd been taking our PAWS group from church to a local nursing home. I contacted the director to tell her what I was doing as an evaluator. I asked her if I might be able to bring the team in training to her site for visits, being fully transparent that we were in the testing phase. She was familiar with the work we were doing with our church's PAWS dogs.

"Hi, Gloria." I introduced myself on the phone. She knew me from PAWS. "I've just become an evaluator for therapy dogs, and I need to find a healthcare setting where I can conduct part of the test. If you'd be open to this, it would be a nice additional opportunity for dogs to visit the residents."

"You already visit at least once a month or more. How is this different?" she asked.

I told her how it would work. "I'll meet with the prospective new therapy dog team somewhere else to do the initial test. When I'm comfortable that the dog is calm and the owner handles the dog well and they've passed a brief obedience type of evaluation, we'd come and do the visit portion of the evaluation in the nursing home."

Gloria hesitated a bit. "Will you and Sadie be with them when they visit? I'm a bit uneasy that they're new to our site and don't know our rules."

"Yes," I assured her, "Sadie and I will be with them. I'll be watching to make sure they're safe as they visit and following all the visit policies we do with PAWS. But for these visits, I'll also be making sure they meet the requirements for the therapy dog test."

There's a portion of the dog test that requires the testing dog to meet a "strange dog," a dog they've not encountered before. I usually used Sadie as the strange dog during this portion of the test. I also used Sadie during the evaluation visits with our testing teams. As I explained to Gloria, it gave me and Sadie a chance to show them how a therapy dog works in this type of setting, how to approach residents and visitors and how to be sociable with other dogs.

"When will you visit and how often will you come?" she asked.

"It'll vary," I responded. "It might be different for each team I'm evaluating. Some people work during the day and those visits will need to be in the evening or on the weekend. You don't need to be there, but I'd like to have a plan to communicate with you so you know we're coming."

Gloria was quiet for a moment, then answered, "I know the staff and residents love the doggy visits. And if you're confident this will be safe, we can make it work. Why don't you just email me and let me know when you're coming."

Things were falling into place. I'd established locations to do the initial test and now had a location to conduct the evaluation visits. Plus I knew the residents and staff would enjoy the extra dog visits.

Over the years, I tested and used this particular healthcare site, as well as a few others, as a testing location for many potential therapy dog teams. It was gratifying to watch the new teams work together and gain confidence in their work.

The frequency with which I did therapy dog evaluations was quite varied. For a time, I'd be busy with two or three teams in a month. Then I'd go a month or two with no evaluations. I evaluated teams interested in therapy dog work in hospitals as well as for other settings, such as schools or libraries, colleges for midterm and finals time, and counseling sessions.

Several employees, visitors and patients who were at one time recipients of the Karing Partners services became a certified therapy dog team. Mary and Sissy came on board because we visited Mary when she was in the hospital, and they stayed active for many years. I evaluated and certified several of the Karing Partner teams, many of whom are still active today.

I received a call one day from a lady who wanted to become part of Karing Partners. "Hi, my name is Vicki. My dog, Audie Murphy, and I want to become part of the therapy dog group you have at the hospital."

"That's great! Tell me a bit about you and your dog. Do you have any basic obedience skills? Do you already have your therapy dog certification?" These were some of my standard questions on that first call.

"We took a class at the local community college, and we have our Canine Good Citizen certificate," she explained. "But I have to be honest, the class went by really fast, and I'm not sure I understand all we need to do to get our therapy dog certificate."

I explained the test process and told her to check online to review what the test entails and the behaviors they'd be testing on. She got back to me a few weeks later.

"I see what we have to do, but I'm still not sure we're ready to do the test," she said, a bit dejectedly.

I told her, "Let's try this. Since you and Audie Murphy are going to become Karing Partners, and since we'll do our testing here at the hospital on the transitional care unit, why don't you come by one day when Sadie and I are visiting and you can see what we do?"

She took me up on my offer. I did this often with teams planning to become part of Karing Partners. Sometimes there would be one or two people that would observe. It was a good use of my time to encourage and explain what the process entailed.

A few days later, Vicki observed as Sadie and I visited. I was able to demonstrate with Sadie what the elements of the test would include and give tips on how we did our visits. By the end of that observation, Vicki and Audie Murphy were ready to set up a date to test.

Vicki and Audie Murphy have been faithful visitors at the hospital for nearly six years. She is also a member of my church. While she was not a member of our PAWS group, Vicki was so excited about her work with therapy dogs, she decided to write an article about the PAWS dogs for a magazine. She put together a gathering of the PAWS ministry group at the nursing home where PAWS routinely visited, along with my husband to take pictures. This particular article was published in *Response: The magazine for Methodist Women in Mission*. She's a seasoned author of numerous magazine articles including therapy dog articles for *The Guide Post* and *The Farmer's Almanac*. Yes, Vicki *loves* her therapy dog work![18]

I also evaluated a few teams from PAWS. I would teach the PAWS class, and then local CGC evaluators tested them for the CGC certificate. The teams then went off on their own. A few came back later and asked me to evaluate them for their therapy dog certificate. Zoey, the little blind Maltese, received her therapy dog certificate in this manner. Today, Connie and Zoey visit local nursing homes and Zoey "reads" with the kids at the library. Another team was Julie, a member of our church, and her labrador Casey. Julie's long-term goal was to start with PAWS and obtain a CGC certificate and then later obtain a therapy dog certificate. Julie is a school psychologist and was invited to bring her dog as part of her counseling work once they were certified. Then there was Judy and her second set of dogs, Zeni and Zeta. Like the others, they completed PAWS and got CGC certificates then later received therapy dog certifications. Much like Julie, Judy had long-term plans to use her dogs as part of her work as a clinical psychologist in health care. I was honored and thrilled to be part of the journey with these ladies and their dogs.

Well, Karen, what do you think? I've taken our love for dogs and am experiencing possibilities I never even dreamed about! This journey with therapy dogs has come from a need to celebrate you, our lives together and our lives apart. And to celebrate those things that will outlive the two of us! And it's not over yet . . .

Paws for Reflection

God intends his people to team up to serve and help each other. The apostle Paul urged the Thessalonians to "encourage one another and build each other up" (1 Thessalonians 5:11). God placed us in a world full of people and expects us to live in community. He does not expect us to work alone but to maintain connection and build each other up.

We need each other to walk the path of life that God has placed before us. The words of Paul in 1 Corinthians 1:10 encourage us to have a common purpose when working with others, for he says, "I appeal to you, brothers and sisters . . . that all of you agree with one another in what you say and that there be no divisions among you." While Paul was writing to the early Christian church to remind them to find a common goal in their work, his teaching can apply to our everyday life. When we are together with others, we are to uphold each other, focus on the topic at hand, and support each other in what we are doing together. It may mean listening to someone who's struggling, providing for a practical need or speaking words of encouragement. We can celebrate successes, offer a prayer for strength in difficulty, or challenge each other to grow in faith. And in everything, we must strive to do what is good for each other.

Are you in community with others in an activity? It may be your church, your neighborhood, activities with your children or others where you can serve those in need. Consider what God tells us: to encourage one another and have a heart toward others. I pray that you are, or will become, the person who others say, "They are good to work with, kind and encouraging and uplifting."

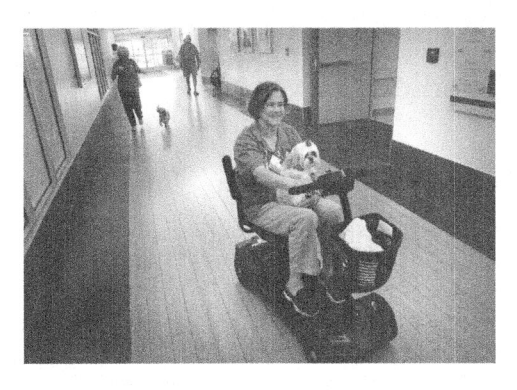

Mary with Sissy (front) and Ruth with Sophie visiting the transitional care unit (Courtesy of the *Pantagraph*)[19]

Chapter 15: Memorable Moments

Helen Keller said, "Alone we can do so little; together we can do so much."[20] A good story is told best when there are many characters. Such is my story; some pieces of it need to be told by others who were part of my years with our therapy dogs. I reached out to a few people who had a significant impact on this work. We laughed and I felt the warmth of Karen's presence as we talked. As I recalled the work we did, I pictured Karen listening and smiling as we talked about our dogs. We knew were doing a good thing, but we all had a different adventure.

Michelle told me her story.

"Overall," she told me, "the thing I'm most proud of is starting the program with you. It's such a feel-good story. I feel like we did something worthwhile and meaningful. I know the intent of the Karing Partners program was for the benefit of patients, but I think there was just as much benefit (if not more) for the staff. I liked hearing how much the staff looked forward to the dog visits. Max brought true joy to the staff. You could feel it and see it. I know he provided stress relief. Often, we made a point to visit specific employees from areas we weren't assigned. The dogs have been missed terribly during the pandemic. Because of COVID, the dog visits are on hold. So people have been asking for months, 'When are the dogs coming back?' That makes me feel so good. It's funny how some people knew Max's name and not necessarily mine. The mental health effects of this pandemic will be the next crisis."

She went on. "From the patient side, the thing I enjoyed most was hearing them say 'You made my day' or 'This has been the best part of my day.' Having a therapy dog visit provided a positive distraction from whatever was going on medically. The pediatric patients in the emergency department [ED] were some of my favorites. The place in the hospital that was always on my heart is the ED. Having worked there for so many years and seeing many sad things, I knew this was a group that would much appreciate the dog visits."

"I remember you saying that, Michelle," I interjected. "I know many of our teams had wonderful and amazing experiences visiting the ED. Do you remember the time you and Max walked a patient out for discharge? I remember thinking what a difference you made to both the patient and the employees that day."

"I do remember that," she said with a chuckle. "You're thinking about Joe."

Joe (not his real name) was one of the many patients in the ED with mental health problems. They frequented the hospital with myriad health complaints, but most were unfounded. Staff would take care of their particular issue for the day and then send them home, knowing they'd be back soon.

Michelle recalled, "Usually Joe was cooperative. But that day was different; Joe didn't want to leave. The doctor treating him saw me and Max and asked if we might be able to help with settling Joe and getting him ready for discharge. I told him we could help but we were volunteers and I couldn't do any of my nursing activities.

"The doctor said he understood. Here's what he proposed: Joe loves dogs, he talked about his dogs all the time, and if we got Joe's permission, Max and I could be in the room with him when they provided discharge instructions and plans to go home. Hopefully, Max would be a calming influence.

"So Max and I went to the room, introduced ourselves and asked if Joe wanted to pet and talk to Max. Joe was quite eager when he saw Max. Max immediately went over to Joe, and Joe was thrilled. I could tell Max was equally delighted by his happy face and wagging tail.

"The doctor and nurse came in with discharge information. The doctor told Joe he was happy to see he was enjoying Max; then told Joe they were ready to send him home.

"I realized that part of the discharge plan was to get Joe on the city bus to get him home. I wondered if it might be easier for Joe if Max and I were part of that," she continued the story. "I went to the doctor and told him I'd be willing to stay with Joe and walk him to the bus. They thought it was a great idea, so that's what we did. When the bus arrived just outside the door, Max and I escorted a calm Joe to the bus with his discharge papers." We laughed as we reminisced.

Then she told me another story.

"We completed our visits one day and were ready to go home. But as we were leaving, I felt a nudge to stop by the emergency department. I just knew something awful had taken place," she recalls. "When I got there, I could feel it in the air. Sadness, tears and grief were everywhere. A young child had been in the ED and they were unable to save him. As I walked in, the nurse who had cared for the child was crying and walked up to me. She asked me if she could take Max to the back room and cry."

Michelle knew the nurse and understood the emotions she was experiencing. "I walked them to the backroom and then let Max and the nurse go in alone. I stood outside the door until the nurse gathered her emotions. When she was ready, the nurse walked out of the room and returned the leash to me and she said, 'You have no idea of what Max's presence here today has meant to me. I don't think I could have returned to my job if you hadn't been here.'" I recall Karing Partner volunteers visiting the ED who encountered similar stories, but none quite as poignant as this.

A study about ED staff looked at therapy dogs and art therapy as stress reducers for doctors and nurses. The researchers looked at the effectiveness of therapy dogs versus coloring versus no intervention (control) in reducing their stress. Participating ED physicians and nurses provided three self-reported assessments of stress and saliva samples before and after their specific stress reducer: dogs, coloring, or nothing. Over 100 staff members participated. Their initial results showed that a five-minute therapy dog interaction was the one that reduced their stress the most.[21]

Michelle finished her story by telling me, "You know, Max died last year. We did almost twelve years of visits. I loved every minute of it. We have a few of the old crew still around and waiting to resume visits. We were approved to start visits last May during Hospital Week, but we had another COVID surge and people didn't feel comfortable coming in. Now that we're set to go again, we have Omicron and record-breaking cases and hospitalizations. Visitor restrictions have been re-instituted. Hope we can start again soon. We all miss the doggie visits."

Thanks, Michelle and Max, for all that you did!

Ruth told me her story.

I contacted Ruth and asked if she had stories she wanted to share. She readily responded, "Yes, I'll tell you my favorites!"

"Early in my therapy dog odyssey, I entered the hospital for what I thought was a routine visit. As I headed to sign in, my path was blocked by a group of hospital visitors. Making our way around the group, Sophie suddenly made an abrupt left turn toward a lady sitting off to the side. There was no way Sophie could have seen this lady through the crowd of visitors. I certainly didn't. I dutifully followed behind, slightly irritated with my dog. The lady started petting Sophie and I began talking to her. She asked me about my therapy dog work. As I turned to leave, the lady said, 'I just found out I have Stage IV cancer. I retired four months ago and had my retirement planned out. I'm waiting for a ride right now to see a specialist. I hope he tells me he can stop it.'"

I didn't recall Ruth ever telling me that story. "That's incredible. Do you think Sophie instinctively knew something about this lady? You hear about dogs that smell cancer. Or did Sophie sense the lady's sadness?" I asked.

"I'll never know. When her ride arrived, she thanked us for taking the time to listen. It was then I realized I'd need to let Sophie take the lead when we visited. Over the years, I learned to follow her lead," Ruth said.

Ruth went on to tell another story. "I don't know if you remember this story, it was my first visit as a Karing Partner. You and Sadie were with us. An elderly lady shuffled by with a walker when we arrived on the unit. A nurse was supporting her and helping with the walker. As they walked by, you introduced Sophie and me to the nurse behind the desk. Just then the patient passed us and you asked if we could walk along. We made conversation with the patient and told her the dogs' names. She didn't say anything. At the end of the hall, the patient sat down in a chair, pointed to Sophie, and said, 'Bring me that dog.' I took Sophie to her and she indicated for me to place Sophie on her lap."

Ruth went on. "Sadie walked up while Sophie was in her lap. The woman acknowledged Sadie and kept petting Sophie. She talked to the dogs and told them all about her life, living on a farm and the dogs she had as a child. We eventually thanked her for visiting with us and prepared to see other patients. The nurse behind the desk stopped us. I thought we were in trouble. She told us what she and the other nurses had just observed. She said the patient had been on the unit for five days. During that entire time, she'd never spoken a word. The nurses were astounded the patient was able to talk, that she talked nonstop to the dogs but would not talk to any of them!" We laughed as she told this story, and we talked about a few other stories we remembered.

Sophie was a headliner in her own right. Ruth and Sophie had an article published about an experience they had when a Code Blue was called. A Code Blue is when someone's heart or breathing stops and there's an urgent need for medical assistance from specialists throughout the hospital. They were visiting another patient on the floor when they heard the Code Blue called overhead. Heading for the elevator to leave and be out of the way, they heard a shout, "The dog! The dog! Bring me the dog!" The plea was coming from a lady sitting near the elevator, visibly upset. It turns out the lady was the mother of the young woman for whom the Code Blue was being called. True to her past experience of knowing when she's needed, Sophie sat on the lady's lap for many hours that afternoon, until other family members arrived.

Ruth said, "Sophie remained fixated on this lady as if she could fully understand everything she was being told." Ruth recalls thinking she was not needed in this interaction; it was definitely a relationship just between Sophie and the lady. Sophie was honored with an article published in the *Alliance of Therapy Dogs* magazine for her noble behavior.[22]

Thanks, Ruth and Sophie, for all that you did!

Judy told me her story.

"When the PAWS classes got started, my husband, Doug, and I became interested. We'd seen the joy that our oldest dog, Mindre, brought to people and how her gentleness helped people overcome dog phobias, but she was too old for this work by the time the classes started. Over the next two years, we placed our young dogs, Kaia first then Kyrie the next year, in the PAWS classes. Both were young when we took them through the training, but with lots of additional work on our part, both dogs passed the training and became PAWS ministers with their CGC certificates."

Judy went on, "Gail, I don't know if you recall, but we were so proud to be part of this ministry with the church and to share the love of our dogs with others."

I replied, "I knew this ministry meant a lot to both of you. And I remember how intense you and Doug were about the training. I'd forgotten they were among the youngest dogs that completed the classes successfully. Do you remember the special service Pastor Hoffman conducted with a dog blessing? I think it was you, Doug and your dogs, me and Max, and then Laurie with Milo. It was amazing to be a part of that special blessing."

"Yes, I do remember," Judy said. Then she went on, "We loved this ministry. After our classes and when we had our certificate, we were ready! Because of the level of activity the dogs could handle and my background as a licensed clinical psychologist, our best fit was working with the kids at The Baby Fold. As you know, the kids who behaved well during the day got the reward of time with the dogs. We'd meet in the gym and the supervisor would bring two children at a time to play with

Kaia and Kyrie. The most rewarding thing was watching the kids, even kids who initially were terrified of dogs, have so much fun with Kaia and Kyrie.

"When Doug died, I thanked God I still had Kaia and Kyrie. They helped me through my grief, even while they were grieving. Every morning, for a year and a half, the first thing Kaia did each morning was to go to his office in our home to look for him. My grief was so heavy, but Kaia and Kyrie gave me a reason and a purpose to get up each day."

I remembered all too well when this happened. Judy and Doug were on a mission trip in Hawaii when Doug died unexpectedly. Another death, another person taken so young, with so much life left to live. One day, many years later, I got a call from Judy.

"Do you remember how surprised you were when I called?" she asked me. "I don't think you knew that Kaia and Kyrie had died. When they died, I knew I was going to get more dogs, and when they were ready, I was going to resume my PAWS ministry."

Just like with her first set of Norwegian Elkhounds, Judy got two more Elkies within a year of each other, Zeta and Zeni. And just as she and Doug had done years before, she brought one dog at a time to become a PAWS minister and also obtained their CGC certificate. This time, however, they went one step further and obtained their therapy dog certifications. She went on to tell me all that she'd done with Zeni and Zeta and her dream of using her dogs as therapeutic intervention in her counseling had become a reality.

"I worked hard to get approval through the clinic where I work to use them officially during my counseling," she told me. "While I waited for that green light, I worked with Zeni and Zeta as hospice volunteers and visited nursing homes. And we're part of a stress-reduction effort at the university that helps students relax before taking their final exams. But my greatest joy is using them in my practice. I have many patients who benefit greatly from Zeni and Zeta's presence. They provide comfort, a healthy distraction from intense therapy work, and have helped to prevent pseudo-seizures in patients who are overwhelmed. If a patient cancels, my dogs and I may visit other medical practices in the building. My colleagues now consider therapy dog day at work the best day of the week because the dogs help them de-stress and experience joy. I feel so blessed to be able to be a hu-*mom* to all my dogs and share the wonder of them with others."

Thanks, Judy and Doug, Kaia and Kyrie, and Zeni and Zeta, for all that you did!

I listened in awe to Judy's story. I was speechless as she told me all she'd accomplished, so much of the dream she'd once told me about, she'd achieved. And to think I'd walked a few of those steps with her brought tears to my eyes. It made me look again at the stories from Michelle and Ruth and my own stories—and all the others with whom I worked as therapy dog teams. What joy we experienced as we reached out with our dogs. What joy those we visited also experienced, all because of doggie smiles, happy tails and all!

Paws for Reflection

Teamwork is the theme here! It's clear from these stories that none of this work was done in isolation. There was never one person who made PAWS or Karing Partners work. It was the combined effort of many people. Those who received our services experienced love and joy only because so many came together to use their gifts and offer their love. These thoughts are supported by Ecclesiastes 4:9–10 (NLT) which tells us, "Two people are better off than one, for they can help each other succeed. If one person falls, the other can reach out and help."

We all have different gifts, abilities and interests. We are charged to honor God by serving others with those gifts. What better way to demonstrate the love of God than by sharing our love with others—and in this case, the love of our dogs. Any time we work together, giving our time and attention to love others, we are using our "spiritual gift ... given to each of us so we can help each other" (1 Corinthians 12:7 NLT).

There are many ways we work with others to serve. Is there a place you can serve on a team doing God's work? In Karing Partners, we found that having just one additional doggie team made a huge positive difference for those we were serving. Is there a team you might be able to become part of? It may be writing letters, visiting the sick, helping with food pantries, doing therapy dog work, etc. Look inside and see what gifts you have been given to use alongside team members to share with others.

Sadie waiting for a walk at Gulf State Park

Chapter 16: Always a Therapy Dog

I was active in therapy dog work for over twenty years until we moved to Fond du Lac, Wisconsin, in the fall of 2019. As soon as we got settled in our new home, I set out to find a venue where we could be active again as a therapy dog team. I found a local hospice organization looking to start a therapy dog program as part of their volunteer activities. I completed the application.

Suddenly, it was spring 2020. COVID-19 had arrived and everything changed. It seemed the world just stopped. Plans for doing volunteer work were put on hold.

It was also a difficult time for those expecting therapy dog visits. Therapy dog associations posted information and encouraged teams to try a variety of methods to keep the dogs active. They encouraged innovative ideas for those willing and able to do some kind of dog visit. It was uplifting to read the creative ways teams "visited," such as video streams of dogs doing activities, FaceTime interactions, and tricks and smiles through the windows.

David and I are fortunate to be the proverbial "snowbirds." We were in southern Alabama when COVID struck, staying in our camper at the time. We decided to delay our return to Wisconsin until late spring when we hoped the virus would be gone.

Sadie was with us, as usual. Sadie came to Gulf Shores, Alabama, for the first time when she was just two years old. We'd walk the trails up to eight miles a day. We'd start our day with a three-mile walk and take a few shorter walks as the day got warmer. Over the years, we've seen deer, alligators, bobcats, and have heard coyotes howl in the distance. Our favorite trails are the grass and sand trails that meander through the forests. In the early years, we walked very fast, as Sadie was in a hurry to get to wherever we were going. But now, as Sadie has passed her twelfth birthday, our walks are slower and consist more of smelling, dare I say smelling the doggie roses—smells only a dog can love, smells of the critters that have roamed overnight or the many dogs that have walked through and left their mark.

Chapter 16: Always a Therapy Dog

During the pandemic, I could tell Sadie missed doing her work. As we walked the trails and roads in the campground, more than ever she was interested in interacting with the people we saw. She engaged quickly with anyone wanting to give her attention and would often lean into them as they were petting her. A good friend once said, "Her name isn't Sadie, her name is Ilene because that's what she does!" I guess, once a therapy dog, always a therapy dog!

In the summer of 2021, life slowly came back to a semblance of "normal." Getting together with friends became more common and acceptable. Our good friends from Minnesota came to visit us for a few days, and we headed to the local downtown farmers' market.

Joe, David and I went to the farmers' market. The guys went off to get coffee and I set off on my own. As I was walking around, I saw a lady with a lovely golden retriever. I walked over to her and asked if I could pet the dog.

"What a lovely dog you have," I said, admiring her companion.

"Thanks. But he doesn't belong to me, he belongs to my daughter. They're living with us during the pandemic. She sold her home in Milwaukee and is living with us for a while. She brought Felix along with her," she explained.

I was petting Felix and I could tell he loved the attention. He was well behaved and accepted my touching him with great delight. Doggie happiness was evident: tail and butt wagging, and he looked me straight in the eyes with a smile on his face.

"How old is he? He's so well behaved," I crooned as I continued to pet him.

"He's six years old. My daughter did lots of training with him. Since they've been living with us, he's mellowed out even more. We have a little dog Oliver, a mini golden doodle. They'd been around each other before but always for short visits. Now that they're together all the time, they're best buds," she went on.

"Have you ever considered Felix becoming a therapy dog? He seems to have the right temperament and you seem outgoing and would make a great team." It had been nearly two years since I'd done a therapy dog evaluation, and at that moment I could tell I was missing it.

She smiled. "I don't think my daughter has time for that kind of thing. But I've been thinking about it for my little dog Oliver. He has a similar temperament, and I think he'd make a great therapy dog."

We chatted for a while about the typical personality of a therapy dog and some of the work and expectations of a therapy dog. We expressed our hopes of the

Chapter 16: Always a Therapy Dog

pandemic being over soon so we could resume fun and good activities, like visits with our therapy dogs.

I could have talked for another hour. A possible therapy dog candidate plus the pure joy of talking about therapy dog work was a recipe for a long conversation. Finally, Joe and David found me. They were ready to head home. I took her name and number and said I'd be in touch.

Over the next few weeks, Wendy and I texted back and forth and set up plans for Oliver's therapy dog testing. The therapy dog website had suggestions for testing during the pandemic. The key was to get the okay ahead of time in the locations we hoped to test.

I called PetSmart to see if we could do our therapy dog test there, and the lady was very accommodating. She was excited to hear there were going to be therapy dog activities again. With Wendy's help, we found a hospice house that would allow us to conduct our remaining evaluation visits.

"I'm happy to hear the dogs are coming again," the lady at PetSmart told me on the phone. "I've missed seeing them. We have a great place to do the test here in the store. We used to host testing teams all the time before COVID." Her voice was upbeat and fast.

On the day of the test, I left Sadie in the car. I'd go and get her for the strange dog portion of the test a bit later. Sadie was used to this; she lay down in the back seat to wait till I came back. I introduced myself to the salesperson and explained what we were doing.

"Not a problem," she said. "I knew you were coming. Come on and I'll show you where you can test. This little closed-off area is where we do all the testing. If you want you can take the dogs through the store when you're done and walk around and see people."

I went back to the front door to wait for Wendy and Oliver. When they walked in, I greeted Oliver. He was happy, happy, happy! Tail and butt wags, tongue hanging out the side of his mouth and panting his joy to see someone and get some rubs.

We walked back to the testing area. After I explained what we were going to do, I reviewed her paperwork. I was pleased she had everything in order. "Are you ready?" I asked.

With that, we proceeded to go through the test. Wendy and Oliver had done some obedience classes and they did well with that portion of the test. When I was convinced that Oliver passed all the initial elements, I explained I'd go and get Sadie and we'd do the strange dog portion of the test.

I brought Sadie in and we did our walk-bys and both dogs behaved well. Oliver was interested, but not overly, in the new dog. Once that was completed, we walked around the store and interacted with customers. This was an essential part of the test: Would Oliver accept strangers touching and petting him? Sadie was in her element doing her therapy dog work! She was a good mentor for Oliver. He caught on quickly and decided he liked all the love he was getting.

After Wendy and Oliver passed their test and first visit evaluation, we had two more visits we needed to complete. Wendy's father was in a hospice house in the local community. She'd spoken with the volunteer director and explained what we were doing. We received permission to bring the dogs in to visit her dad and any employees interested in interacting with the dogs. They'd had an active therapy dog program before the pandemic, but none had visited for almost a year and a half. When we arrived, we were greeted with great enthusiasm.

"Look! The dogs are back!" We were greeted with cheerful welcomes. We couldn't see their smiles behind the masks, but we heard them in their voices. After explaining why we were there and who gave us approval, we were escorted to the volunteer manager's office.

"We're so happy to see you and the dogs," Jenny exclaimed cheerfully as she greeted us. "It almost feels like things are getting back to normal, whatever that is anymore! Go ahead and visit with your dad for as long as you like. You can visit any of the employees. I told them you'd be here today."

As we walked to her dad's room, we visited with the employees on our route. The dogs did a delightful job of interacting with the staff. I watched Oliver and he seemed to enjoy the attention. *He'll make a great therapy dog*, I thought. When we arrived at her dad's room, Wendy's dad and her brother, who was visiting, were pleased to see us.

We met the following week and repeated our activity. I could tell Sadie loved being active again. She sat so nice at home as I changed her collar to her special therapy dog collar and placed a scarf around her neck, just like old times! I swear I saw a lift in her step as we approached the entry of the hospice house. We met Oliver and Wendy in the lobby and traced our steps again to her dad's room. We stopped and loved on employees on our way to her dad's room. Oliver did a fine job, and I signed them off as a full-fledged therapy dog team.

"Wendy, I want to thank you for the opportunity you gave me and Sadie. The chance to resume our therapy dog work has been extremely gratifying."

"I've enjoyed doing this with you and Sadie. I know Oliver's liked it too. We're very excited to be an official therapy dog team," she replied with a smile in her voice.

Chapter 16: Always a Therapy Dog

During our visits to the hospice house, the volunteer manager approached me about becoming a therapy dog volunteer. I thought back to the agency I'd considered for therapy dog work a year before. I'd taken a very part-time position there as a hospice RN. They did not allow being both an employee and a volunteer, so I said yes to the hospice house. I was ready to return to therapy dog work!

Sadie and I completed our volunteer application and orientation. We made three visits before our departure as snowbirds to Gulf Shores for the winter. Jenny, the volunteer manager, was aware we were heading south and only able to do only a few visits. We assured her we'd be back in the spring. I smiled as I thought about how good it felt to be getting back into therapy dog work. I told Sadie what we were going to do and I think I saw her smile. Once a therapy dog, always a therapy dog!

Today, Sadie and I walked our favorite trail in Gulf State Park. The weather is lovely. Sixty degrees and sunny with a clear, bright blue sky. It's a perfect day to be outside and be active. Not too hot. Our walk requires me to wear a light, long-sleeved shirt and long pants. Even though she just passed her twelfth birthday, she still loves her walks. When she sees her halter that we use for walks and her leash, she quickly gets up and stretches—a sure sign of an upcoming walk. The walk today is slower than it used to be and more *smelly*. We stop at least every six feet to check out another doggie-lovin'-only smell. The light of the sun radiates through the tall long-leaf pine trees and the palms. We hear birds in the background, and if we listen hard, we can hear the water from the Gulf of Mexico slap onto the shore. It's windy, so the waves are active, and the trees are beautiful as they gently sway with the wind. A little bit of heaven right here. How blessed I am!

My thoughts wander as Sadie and I walk, and I think about the past twenty-five years. How I miss Karen. I dream about what might have been. We were so close. We'd talked about living together as old ladies; how we'd take care of each other and our dogs just like we did as kids. Ah, dreams. Here I am today, an old lady. But without her. I picture her looking down at us from her place in heaven. I think about the work I've done in her memory. I think she's pleased. As long as it involved dogs, Karen was happy. I thank God again for the joy he has placed in my life. Is it okay to feel sadness and think about joy at the same time? Maybe that's what life is about. A mixture of good and bad, happy and sad. It's simply the finding it that takes a lifetime.

Paws for Reflection

> How long, Lord? Will you forget me forever?
> How long will you hide your face from me?
> How long must I wrestle with my thoughts
> And day after day have sorrow in my heart?
> How long will my enemy triumph over me?
>
> Look on me and answer, Lord my God.
> Give light to my eyes, or I will sleep in death,
> and my enemy will say, "I have overcome him,"
> and my foes will rejoice when I fall.
>
> But I trust in your unfailing love;
> my heart rejoices in your salvation.
> I will sing the Lord's praise,
> for he has been good to me.
> (Psalm 13)

I rejoice in knowing I will see Karen again. Looking back, I see how so many things have come together in ways I never could have imagined. Possibilities beyond my wildest dreams became realities. The grief I experienced presented me with a journey that helped me find meaning in and through my grief. Only God can take such a time as this—a time of great sadness, loss and grief—and ultimately turn it into joy.

Luke 6:21 says, "Blessed are you who hunger now, for you will be satisfied. Blessed are you who weep now, for you will laugh." It certainly did not feel like it at the time, but as I look back, I see how God led me to the peace and acceptance I now experience. "Peace I leave with you; my peace I give you. I do not give to you as the world gives. Do not let your hearts be troubled and do not be afraid" (John 14:27).

Look around you. Have you asked God to be part of your life? That good and also that sad part of your life? Please open your heart to accept his invitation to know him better, to establish a personal relationship with God. Once you have a personal relationship with the Lord, he will help you align your gifts and desires.

May there be, for you, opportunities in your life to turn losses and grief into times of joy and celebration. Into beautiful possibilities beyond your wildest dreams. Shalom.

Becoming a Therapy Dog Team

Have you ever thought about becoming part of a therapy dog team?

Do you and your dog have what it takes?

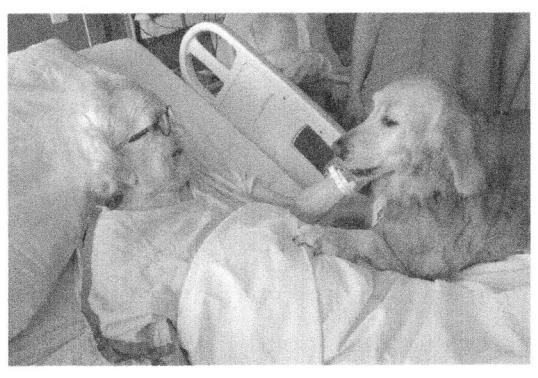

Max accepts an invitation to get up close and personal
(Courtesy of the Pantagraph)

I'd like to give you some information as you ponder the idea of becoming a therapy dog team.

Click on the link below to find out more.

And, while you are there—test yourself on some key elements about therapy dog visits in a hospital

https://pawspurpose.net/paws-purpose-giveaway/

Now It's Your Turn!

Thank you for reading my book! I hope you enjoyed reading it as much as I enjoyed telling it!

Please do me a favor and go to Amazon and leave me a review. I value your input! This helps other people, like yourself, find this book and share with others.

Thank you so much!

What's Next?

Gail is currently working on her next book, Paws, *Purpose, and (more) Possibilities*, which will be about therapy dogs (of course!) and will be dedicated to healthcare professionals.

Please visit her website to share your own stories about the impact your therapy dog work has had on those in hospitals, emergency situations, hospice, nursing homes and other health care situations so your story can be considered for the book.

See my web page for more information on therapy dogs, books and other resources about therapy dogs:
https://pawspurpose.net/

A portion of all book royalties is donated to charity. For a list of the charities, please see my website.

Acknowledgments

I want to thank many who helped make this book a reality. First and foremost, thanks to my husband, David, who's been a perpetual source of encouragement and support through it all, from living it to writing about it. He has been my strongest voice of encouragement and tolerance. I am so proud to display his wonderful photographic gifts in this book, which add so much to the story! Thanks to my niece, Shannon, for whom this story brings back tearful memories but who supported me in telling her mom's story. And to Shannon's daughter, Karen's granddaughter, Eva, who provided creative phrases to my book. And of course, to my dogs and all the people and therapy dogs who together made this book a story.

Thanks to my beta readers for reviewing the book many times and providing quality input to help make the book better for the reader: my husband, David; my cousins Vicki Roehrig and Doug Hanneman; David's niece Debbie Disher and husband Mike Disher. Vicki brought a personal side to the review, as she was there in person or by phone for almost every story; Doug used his background as a newspaper editor; Debbie provided insight from her background in education and library sciences; Mike brought his skills as a man of details. All of them brought their faith in God and their willingness to go above and beyond! *Thank you* just doesn't say enough!

My work with Self-Publishing School coaches and other students is much appreciated. Coach Kerk was very supportive and gave great suggestions and kept me on track; and many of the new friends and students I met on the SPS Facebook were instrumental in their feedback, encouragement and their personal stories. Many thanks to editor Carly Catt for her diligent work to bring the book to its point of being ready for publication. And thanks to Alejandro Martin for his attention to the design and formatting to make this book one I am proud to publish!

A special thanks to those who were in places and served in roles that allowed so many good things to take place. A special thank you to Cindy at The Baby Fold, where I started my adventure with my dogs, and whose

Acknowledgments

support for the kids she worked with made a difference in their lives. A special thanks to Kathy and others who provided many years of CGC evaluations for the PAWS classes. I thank all of those I mentioned and failed to mention (sorry!) who were pivotal in making this work a reality.

This book could not be written without the mention of so many who were part of Karing Partners and PAWS. My apologies to any I missed on my list, but you are in my heart. Tammy and Bear. Lisa and Bella. Randy and Lacy. Courtney and Dailey. Michelle and Max. Gary and Max. Pam and Marilyn and Cheetah. Mary and Lucy. Kathy and Ebbie. Laura and Moose. Ruth and Sophie. Mary and Sissy. Nancy with Zeke, Rudy and Sadie Ann. Jim and Cooper. Katie and CeCe. Bobbie and Reilly. Vicki and Audie Murphy. Penny and Howie. Bill and Bailey. Christine and Ranger. Brittany and Mary Kay. Jacqui and Charley. Paula and Hannibal. Patti and Mimi. Doug and Judy with Kaia, Kyrie, Zeta and Zeni. Lori and Milo. Jean and Claire. Mary and Toby. Lisa and Milo. Ken and Sally with Gizmo, Bailey and Oreo. Dan and Boca. Darcy and Lizzy. Valerie and Parker. Marcia and Amber. Dave and PJ. Eric and Tammy with Holly. Amy and Maddie. Carolyn and Sophie. Pastor Camilla and Carmel. Linda and Benson. Gary and Murphy. Jim and Miles. Myla and Gus. Jayne and Gus. Melinda and

Brandy. Pastor Vaughn and Kate. Jim and Eddie. Larry and Hannah. Becky and Duke. Brittany and Enzo. Meagan and Lucca. Michelle and Charlie. Brita and Dallas. Connie and Zoey.

Author Bio

Gail has spent a lifetime loving her family and her dogs. As a registered nurse, she's worked in a variety of areas in the hospital, in home care and in hospice. She also taught nursing students for twenty years. Since retiring, she's resumed part-time work in hospice. Gail combines her personal and professional experiences when working with therapy dogs and those in hospice.

Gail earned a bachelor of science degree in nursing at Bowling Green State University, and a master of science in nursing at Northern Illinois University. In her various roles working throughout the Midwest, Gail did program development, created and wrote professional documents, presented at professional conferences, and authored and co-authored professional articles. This is her first book.

Gail currently resides with David, her husband of nearly forty-four years, and Sadie, her third golden retriever and therapy dog, in Wisconsin. Her hobbies include snow birding in Gulf Shores, AL, during the cold Wisconsin winters, traveling, gardening, therapy dog work and spending time with family and friends.

Endnotes

1	Christina Gregory, "The Five Stages of Grief: An Examination of the Kubler-Ross Model, PSYCOM (website), April 14, 2022, https://www.psycom.net/depression.central.grief.html.
2	Paul Swiech, "Therapy dogs comfort patients," *The Pantagraph,* September 16, 2016, page D1.
3	Gabriel Fledman, "5 Advantages for kids who grow up with dogs," The Drake Center (blog), April 7, 2017, https://www.thedrakecenter.com/services/dogs/blog/5-advantages-kids-who-grow-dogs.
4	Roger A. Caras, QuotesWave.com, accessed May 17, 2022, https://www.quoteswave.com/text-quotes/123056.
5	Canines for Christ (website), accessed May 6, 2022, https://k9forchrist.org/.
6	Talitha McLachlan, "21 wise and elegant Charles Dickens quotes for teachers," HOPE (blog), accessed May 17, 2022, https://blog.hope-education.co.uk/charles-dickens-quotes/.
7	Sabrina Schuck, "Therapy dogs effective in reducing symptoms of ADHD, study finds," *Science News,* University of California, July 18, 2018, https://www.sciencedaily.com/releases/2018/07/180718170258.htm.
8	"Top reasons to adopt a pet," Humane Society of the United States (website), accessed May 6, 2022, https://www.humanesociety.org/resources/top-reasons-adopt-pet.

9   "Certified Therapy Dog—Get Your Therapy Dog Certification," Alliance of Therapy Dogs (website), May 23, 2017, https://www.therapydogs.com/therapy-dog-certification/.

10   "How Humans Can Learn From Dogs," Cesar's Way (blog), June 25, 2019, https://www.cesarsway.com/how-humans-can-learn-from-dogs/.

11   Paul Swiech, "Unleash a dog's love," *The Pantagraph*, November 22, 2004, page C1.

12   Anna Gawlinkski and Neil Steers, "**Animal Assisted Therapy & What Science Says**," UCLA Health (website), November 15, 2005, https://www.uclahealth.org/pac/animal-assisted-therapy.

13   Paul Swiech, "Therapy dogs comfort patients," D1.

14   Mayo Clinic Staff, "Pet Therapy: Animals as healers," Consumer Health, *Mayo Clinic Healthy Lifestyle,* September 15, 2020, https://www.mayoclinic.org/healthy-lifestyle/consumer-health/in-depth/pet-therapy/art-20046342.

15   Maya Angelou, "Maya Angelou: How You Made Them Feel," Notewothy Nonsense, March 31, 2022, https://noteworthynonsense.com/blog/08/2020/Maya-Angelou-How-You-Made-Them-Feel.

16   Gail Scoates, "Investigate biosocial changes after a Karing Partner/dog therapy visit," (unpublished manuscript, June 2016), typescript.

17   James Herriot, Quotefancy.com, accessed May 17, 2022, https://quotefancy.com/quote/3004373/James-Herriot-There-have-been-times-in-my-life-when-confronted-by-black-and-hopeless.

18   Vicki Cox, "The four-footed ministry of Gail Scoates," *Response: The Magazine of Women in Mission*, United Methodist Women, July/August 2019, page 16-17.

19   Paul Swiech, "Therapy dogs comfort patients," D1.

20   Helen Keller, BrainyQuote.com, accessed May 17, 2022, https://www.brainyquote.com/quotes/helen_keller_382259.

21   Jeffrey A. Kline, et al., "Randomized Trial of Therapy Dogs Versus [Art Therapy] to Reduce Stress in Emergency Medicine Providers," *Academic Emergency Medicine: A Global Journal of Emergency Care 27,* no. 4 (April 2020): 266–275, https://doi.org/10.1111/acem.13939.

22   Ruth Davidson, "Sophie," *Alliance of Therapy Dogs 10*, no. 1 (2015).

Made in the USA
Monee, IL
14 June 2022